Ken Garland

Mr Beck's Underground Map

Capital Transport

Map into Diagram

Though not strictly speaking a map, this term is almost universally used by people when referring to the London Underground Diagram, hence the title of this book. Throughout the text however, the more accurate word diagram is used with a capital D to distinguish it from other maps of the same subject.

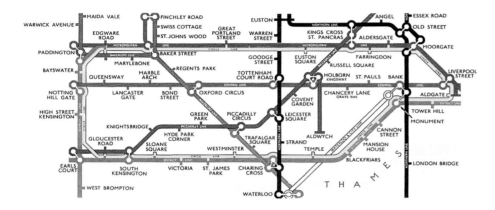

Poster and card folder sizes

By far the most common size for the poster was, and still is, quad royal; 40 x 50in (1016 x 1270mm). This was the size most commonly used by the main line railway companies for their general publicity posters. Underground companies used double royal, 40 x 25in (1016 x 635mm), for the majority of their general publicity posters, while maintaining the quad royal size for the Diagram (as they did for geographical maps of the Underground network which were also displayed at their stations). Beck card folder sizes varied slightly over the years, from as small as 5½ x 8in (140 x 203mm) to as large as 6 x 9in (152 x 229mm). They were folded twice on the long edge to produce a pocketable object of about 6 x 3in (152 x 76mm).

First published 1994
Reprinted 1998
Reprinted 2003

ISBN 185414 168 6

Published by Capital Transport Publishing
38 Long Elmes, Harrow Weald, Middlesex

Designed by Ken Garland and Associates

Printed by C S Graphics, Singapore

Contents

Acknowledgements

I am much indebted to the following for their painstaking comments on my text: Doug Rose, Alan Blake, Mike Horne, Jonathan Roberts, George Jasieniecki and Tim Demuth; without their generous help I would have committed some errors, both of commission and omission. Of course any errors still remaining are entirely my own responsibility. I am equally indebted to Paul E Garbutt and to Bryce Beaumont for the reminiscences that they shared with me in our meetings, and to the latter for giving permission to reproduce here, as one of the appendices, a hitherto unpublished memoir of his friend and colleague, Harry Beck. Beck's niece, Joan Baker, shared her fond memories of him with me, for which I am most grateful. Thanks are due to Mark Dennison, Curator, Patricia Austin, Librarian and Jonathan Riddell, Map Librarian, all of London Transport Museum, for their invaluable help. I am happy to record here my appreciation of the dedicated collaboration of my colleagues, Colin Bailey and Richard Marston, in the design of the book and for many helpful suggestions in the compilation of material. Lastly, and not least, my especial thanks to Herbert Spencer for first persuading me to write on the subject, back in 1969, and to Jim Whiting for encouraging me to expand my earlier piece into the present work.

The author and publisher are grateful to London Transport Museum and London Regional Transport for permission to reproduce the maps and diagrams included in this work.

Foreword

Andrew J. Scott, Director of the London Transport Museum 1988-94;
Director of the National Railway Museum from 1994.

By the time I joined the London Transport Museum as its Director in 1988, I was aware of just what a seminal piece of design we were privileged to safeguard in the Museum's map collections.

As a young child in the 1950s, the Underground Diagram had been part of the fascination of a trip to London. Collecting pocket maps – Journey Planners, as we must now call them – enabled even the untrained schoolchild to appreciate the unique and subtle qualities of this piece of graphic design. However, it wasn't until many years later that I began to discover the story of the person behind the name 'H.C. Beck' which was to be found in the bottom left hand corner of each map.

Ken Garland's work provides us with new insights into the man who created this 'Design Classic'. First, as one who became a close friend and confidant of Beck's, Ken Garland is uniquely well placed to provide us with a feeling for the man and his personality. Second, in the correspondence which punctuated Beck's ultimately doomed relationship with London Transport, we can see just how closely Beck identified with his creation. Perhaps most importantly, we can see in some of Beck's development sketches and experiments, the great care and, indeed, the near obsessive zeal, with which he continued to develop his design.

The London Underground Diagram has achieved the status of a defining icon of information design. Its continuing ability to take adaptation to meet the changing needs of travellers, whilst retaining its essential character, is perhaps its most enduring characteristic. Ken Garland's text makes it clear that change was an essential element of Beck's work. This is not an example of a single brilliant creation but a concept which was constantly moulded and shaped at its creator's hand for nearly thirty years.

The presentation sketch now in the collections of the London Transport Museum provides evidence that change started early. At about the time that Beck was making his first presentation of the Diagram, in the summer of 1931, the Piccadilly Line's Down Street station closed. Close examination of the sketch shows that Down Street has been erased and neighbouring stations re-spaced to fill the gap. One is tempted to imagine Beck's sense of humour being severely tested by a last minute adjustment prior to its submission, but this can only be speculation!

The process of change continues. It is a further mark of the brilliance of Beck's basic concept that, in recent years, it has survived digitisation and transfer to a computer aided design system, together with the addition of the Docklands Light Railway and the Jubilee Line extension. That these changes have been accommodated so successfully is also a mark of London Underground's awareness of the importance of the design in its charge. The Underground Diagram is more than a simplification of Underground railway routes. For most Londoners, it is an essential simplification of the city itself. Long may it continue to be an essential part of London life.

Chapter 1

A Timely Image

Though conceived as no more than a common-sense device intended to help Tube travellers to get on at the right station, make the right connections and get off at the right destination, the London Underground Diagram quickly became more than that. Over the last 60 years many newcomers to London, whether as visitors or residents, have pounced on the Diagram as on a magic guide to a hitherto totally bewildering city. Before them was an orderly simulacrum for a disorderly, disjointed accumulation of urban villages, only barely discernible from one another on the ground, yet possessed with all the pride and exclusiveness of true communities: Camden Town, Hammersmith, Lambeth, Hampstead, Kensington, Acton, Barking, Aldgate, Bayswater... What matter if Chelsea was nowhere to be seen in its orderly array, nor Bloomsbury, nor Mayfair, nor Bermondsey? They'd be fitted into the newcomer's mental map sooner or later, once the basic linkage had been absorbed and its litany learned; for example, that Leicester Square was 'below' Tottenham Court Road, Oxford Circus to its 'left', Goodge Street 'above' it and Holborn to its 'right'.

Critics protested that the Diagram was an inaccurate and misleading guide to London's complex configuration; some were even suspicious of its real purpose, hinting that it might be part of a devious plot to fool a gullible public into thinking the remoter stations on the Underground were more accessible than in fact they were*.

But the public knew better on both grounds. They were not under any illusion about the city's real nature; after all, they had walked, even if briefly, along its irregular streets unsure whether they were going east, or north, or possibly west. They knew very well that London was not a grid city, like New York, or a radial city, like Paris, but one to which no easy handle could be applied. And even the most experienced of them could not tell you where its centre was:

Trafalgar Square? Piccadilly Circus? Parliament Square? Marble Arch? Hyde Park Corner? Saint Pauls? The only possible answer was, all of these and none of these. How could a conglomeration cobbled together from the space between the two historic entities, the Cities of London and Westminster, bring itself to choose one indisputable focal point?

The Diagram reflected this in its unemphatic display of the central area, roughly bounded by the Inner Circle (later the Circle Line), where no single feature was dominant. Equally important, in order to achieve a clear, comprehensive array of features within this central area, it had to be enlarged in relation to the outlying regions. Distortion was thus of the essence. But whereas distortion may often be whimsical, devious or just plain inept, this was purposeful, straightforward and skilful. Furthermore, it represented a view of London and its Underground that people had — albeit unconsciously — been looking out for. One that would cope with the information needs of a growing population now committed to travelling considerable distances to work every day from the new suburbs†, and of visitors from the provinces making their first, timorous acquaintance with the metropolis in increasing numbers throughout the 1930s.

Above any consideration of the Diagram as a navigation aid was the optimistic vision it offered of a city that was not chaotic, in spite of appearances to the contrary, that knew

---

* Appearing in a documentary on the Diagram mounted by BBCtv as part of their Design Classics series, the design historian Adrian Forty commented: 'The point about the map was that it made those outlying stations seem relatively close to the centre of London. The prospect of making a journey to Cockfosters or Ruislip, if one had looked at a geographically correct map, would have seemed rather formidable. Looking at the Underground map, it looks reasonably simple.'

† London's population increased by 1.5 million between the wars. Rides per head of population on London's buses, trams, tubes and trains rose from 259 per year in 1911 to 443 in 1938/39. (Information taken from Weightman and Humphries, *The Making of Modern London 1914-1939*. London 1984).

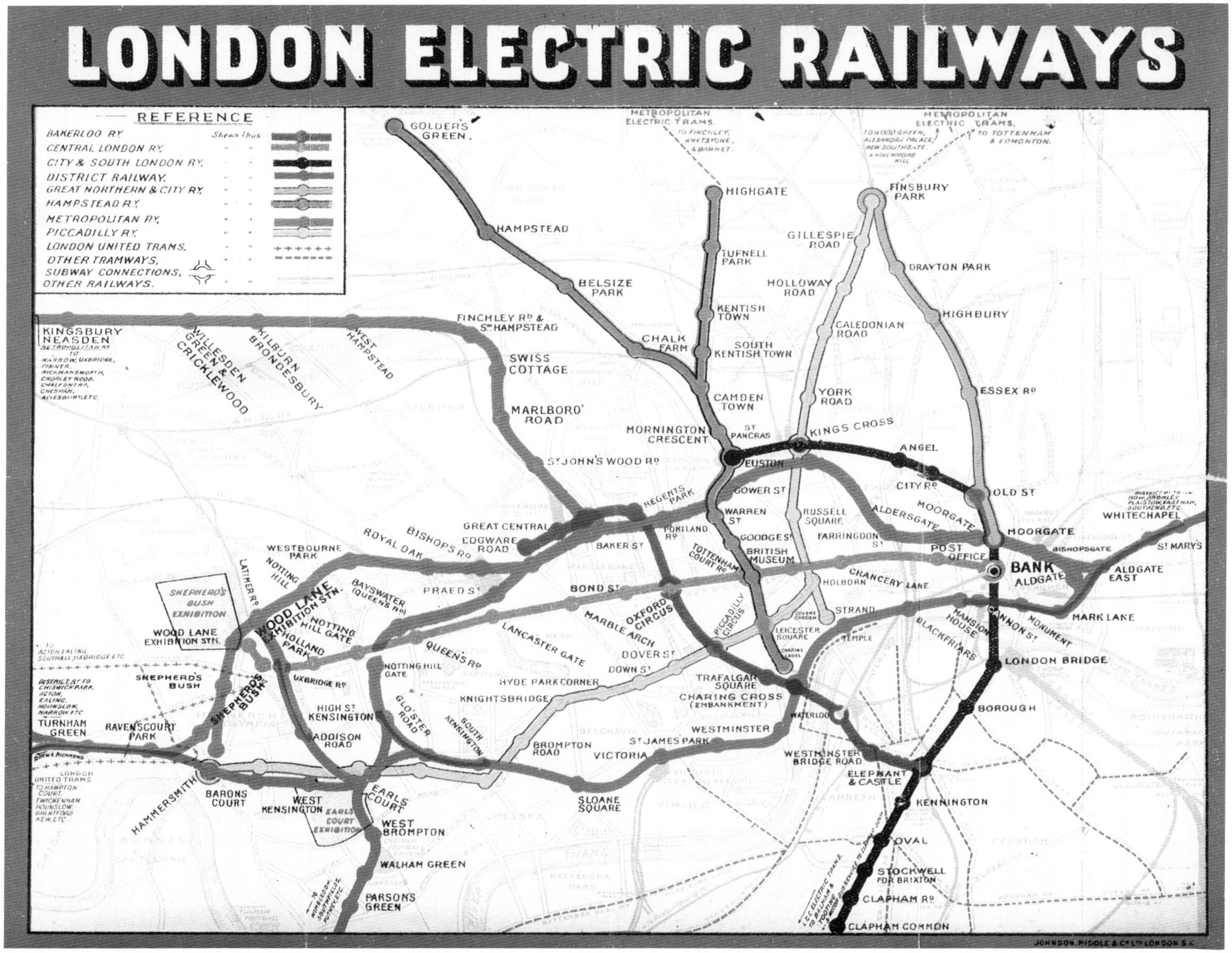

LONDON ELECTRIC RAILWAYS

1 Following maps published in 1906 of the main group of four underground railways, the first all-inclusive map was published in 1908 in the style shown here. Note that, although the map appears to be an accurate geographical representation, it is not so: the Metropolitan Railway route from West Hampstead is distorted to run due west and make space for the key directly above it.

2 Map of the Metropolitan Railway, 1923, showing connections with the District Railway and the tube lines. Comparison with the general map of 1908 (p 8) will show that the latter included only the inner portions of the Metropolitan, which at this time extended over the Chiltern Hills to Aylesbury and beyond, to the two branches terminating at Verney Junction and Brill. There was even more geographical distortion on this map than on the 1908 general map; the outlying parts of the line were considerably compressed (see accurate map in Appendix H).

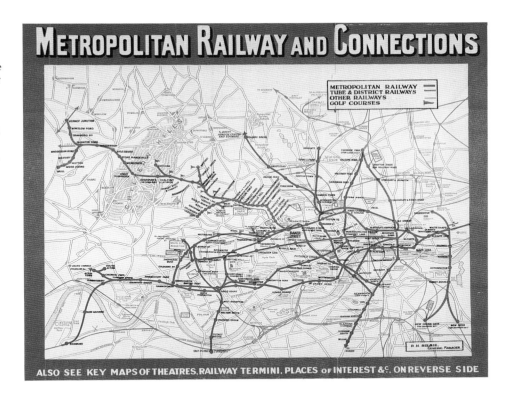

what it was about and wanted its visitors to know it, too. Its bright, clean and colourful design exuded confidence in every line. Get the hang of this, it said, and the great metropolis is your oyster.

However did they all manage to get along before it burst on their delighted gaze?

Before the Diagram

Combined maps of London's underground railways began to be issued for passengers in 1906, when those under the control of an American financier, Charles Tyson Yerkes, were brought together on one map. Though Yerkes died in 1906 his expansionist plans were pursued with vigour by his successors. The following year, agreement between his company, the Underground Railways of London (UERL), and the competing Central London, Metropolitan, Great Northern & City, and City & South London Railways *, led, among other things, to publication of the first all-inclusive map. The finances of some of these companies were in a

parlous state (none of the three new tube lines opened by UERL in 1906-7 was performing up to expectation, in spite of extensive publicity) and a measure of co-operation on fares and other matters was seen as essential to their joint survival. In 1907 they agreed to promote their joint interests as 'a complete system of underground railways' with the trading name 'Underground'. Another company, the Waterloo & City, decided not to participate, though its line was nevertheless shown on several Underground maps between 1908 and 1913. The first general map, issued in 1908 (**1**), was admirable in its intention and no doubt very helpful to the hard pressed traveller; but it presented an illusion of unity

* Given here are the names of the UERL companies as they were in December 1907. They were later to become known as (respectively) the District, Piccadilly, Bakerloo, and Northern. The Central London Railway became known as the Central Line from 1937; the City & South London was absorbed into the Northern in effect from the mid 1920s and by name in 1937; and the Great Northern & City (part of BR from 1976) was renamed the Northern City in 1934. The Metropolitan retained its name unchanged, of course, though even that was temporarily conjoined with the District between 1937 and 1948, sharing the latter's green colour for its route line on the Diagrams at this time.

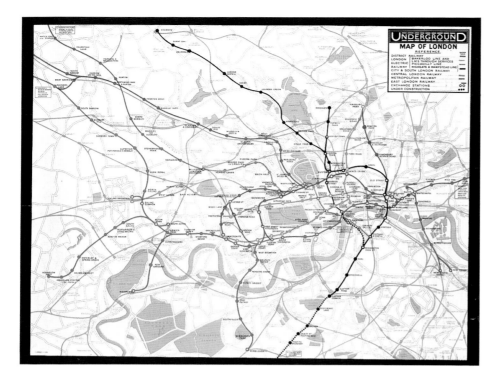

which did not at that time exist. In fact, it must be said that it masked the confused result of largely unplanned development and intense competition.

A series of maps produced by the Metropolitan Railway (**2**) showed its own lines in a strong plum-red and all the others in an undifferentiated blue, and omitted the distinctive logotype employed on maps of the whole network. On this railway at least, a considerable measure of independence was still being maintained in the display of information — and indeed it remained so into the early 1930s. Incidentally, this map vividly illustrates a serious problem confronting cartographers of the Underground, since the Metropolitan Railway extended to the northwest over the Chilterns and beyond Aylesbury to link with the London & North Western Railway at Verney Junction and to Brill on the other branch. Was this extension to be regarded as an integral part of the Underground network, as the map appeared to suggest? Surely not; and in fact it did not appear in its entirety on any general maps of the Underground. Poster maps issued in 1926 and 1927 (**3,4**) for example, do

3,4 Two quad royal maps of 1926 (top, with large border not shown) and 1927 (below), displaying the expanding network. Already, the cartographer was in difficulties with the complexities of the central area. In the 1927 map, the addition of symbols to denote the main line railway terminals, though undertaken with the best of intentions, created a most unhelpful confusion.

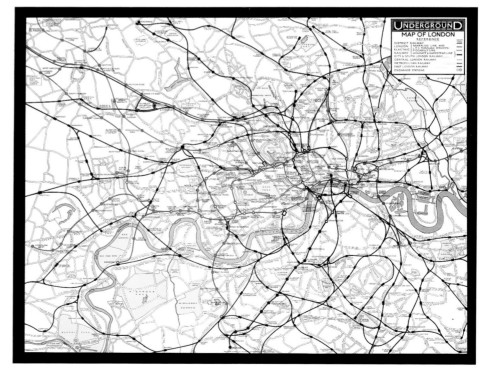

not show, or refer to, any part of that route beyond North Harrow; and other maps (including Beck's first published Diagram of 1933) only indicate the extension as far as Rickmansworth or Aylesbury, although trains continued to run to Verney Junction right up to 1936. Similarly, the District Railway ran a service to Southend until 1939. It appears there was no firm understanding as to where the limits of the Underground network were to be set — at any rate, as far as they were expressed in the authorised map. The fact that such portions of the Metropolitan as that between Harrow and Verney Junction were jointly operated with a main-line company (the Great Central) no doubt complicated the issue. It has to be said that the apparently self-contained nature of the Underground system, symbolised by the 1908 and all successive maps, had the effect of 'freezing out'* the main-line companies, however diligently the Underground Group indicated interchanges with main-line termini.

Even with a truncated map, cut off at North Harrow to the west and Bow Road to the east, as in a 1926 version, the car-tographer was hard put to make sense of the intricate web of connections in the central area; and when a determined effort was made, in a version dated 1932 (**5**), to show the District Railway's route eastward as far as Barking, the complexities of the central area became too small in scale and too jumbled to be of much use to the traveller. However, a card folder series dating from 1926 (**6**), bearing the initials of F H Stingemore, a draughtsman with the Underground Group, incorporated a device which is of considerable interest in relation to the Beck Diagram: he engaged in some topographical distortion whereby outlying portions of the routes were compressed in comparison with the central area. Though he must have realised it would be virtually impossible to present the traveller with a sensible map in pocket size format unless he employed such a device, it may be supposed that, as a traditional cartographer, he undertook it somewhat reluctantly.

* The writer is indebted to Mike Horne for this phrase, and for a number of helpful comments on the development of the Underground during this period.

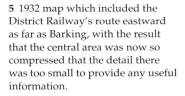

5 1932 map which included the District Railway's route eastward as far as Barking, with the result that the central area was now so compressed that the detail there was too small to provide any useful information.

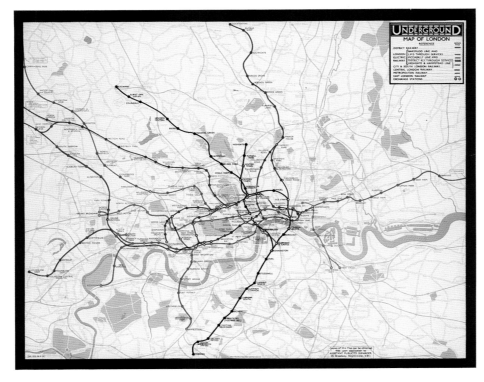

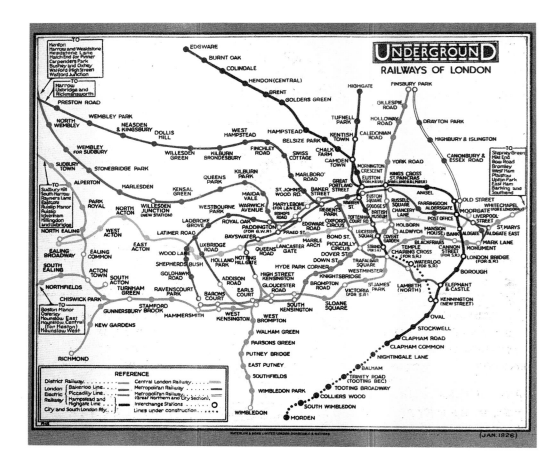

6 F H Stingemore's card folder of
January 1926 very similar in style to
the first edition in the series, published in 1925. A valiant effort to
make the network more compre-
hensible, by means of some com-
pression of the outlying portions
and the removal of surface detail.
It was only partially successful.

route maps; and close inspection reveals that very few of the
Underground maps of the period were really accurate to
scale.

Another feature of Stingemore's card folder series of 1925
is the elimination of all surface detail. This undoubtedly
assists its clarity, though there remains some unfortunate
ambiguity in regard to the central area: it is easy to confuse
Tottenham Court Road and Oxford Circus stations, and
equally easy to confuse Oxford Circus, Leicester Square and
Covent Garden stations. Stingemore must have been made
aware of this, since by the 1932 edition of the card folder (7)
he had amended it so as to expand the area round these
stations. This allowed the station lettering more space and
reduced the possibility of confusion — another instance of
discreet geographical distortion.

Further comparison between figures 6 and 7 shows one
other important modification: in the earlier design there was
no representation of the River Thames, whereas there was in
the later design. It has been established that the river was
omitted on the Stingemore card folders from their inception
in 1925 until April 1926, from which time it was consistently
shown on card folders until the last Stingemore edition of
1932. The exclusion of surface detail from Underground
maps was a gradual, not a sudden, development. A paper
pocket map of c.1909, headed 'London Electric Railways' (of
which a detail is shown in figure 8) had already reduced
streets and other features such as surface railways to faint,
barely legible markings; though it did show tramways and
surface railways; a card folder of c.1912 (already mentioned
in the previous column) excluded streets and surface railways but included the Royal parks and the River Thames;
and a series of maps drawn by the calligraphic artist Mac-
Donald Gill and published in the early 1920s excluded all
surface detail, even the River Thames. It is reasonable to
suppose that these examples were available to Stingemore
and, subsequently, to Beck.

At this point the writer has to confess to an error in his
earlier account* of the development of the Diagram, in
which it was implied (though not expressly stated) that Beck
had invented the 'white-line connector' symbol for interchange stations; but this was not so, since a map by an unknown hand (8), headed 'London Electric Railways' of

* Garland, K, 'The design of the London Underground diagram', *The Penrose
Annual 62*, London 1969.

In the light of this delicate, almost surreptitious, distortion
it is of interest that the very first general Underground map
of 1908 contained a geographical distortion to which no
great objection seems to have been raised, since it reappears
in a paper map dated 1909 and a card folder c.1912: the
Metropolitan Railway's line to Aylesbury was 'redirected'
due west from West Hampstead, instead of curving northwest. Clearly, this was done in order to accommodate a
reference panel in the top left of the map. Here, within a
context of orthodox map-making, is an example of an
Underground route being straightened into a horizontal,
23 years before the design of the Diagram. While it is not
suggested that this example set a conscious precedent for
Beck's proposal, it does indicate a tolerance for, and acceptance of, geographical inaccuracy in relation to Underground

c.1909, clearly shows exactly the white-line connector (as, indeed, does the c.1912 pocket map already referred to). But in any case we shall see later that the white-line connector may not have been considered to be a useful device from about 1912 since it does not reappear until Beck's Diagram of 1946. As for links with main line stations, these were not indicated in some wall maps of 1926 or 1932 (**3**, **5**), but were given special significance in a wall map of 1927 (**4**). Though titled 'Underground map of London' it does in fact incorporate main line routes into London, their stations differentiated by the use of rectangles. The result is confusing and

unhelpful, especially as no reference is made in the key box to these main line route indications (surely an oversight?).

The problems of representing the increasing complexity and expansion of the network were becoming acute by the early 1930s. Stingemore's efforts, though resourceful and well intentioned, provided no more than a partial answer. It was high time for a more drastic solution.

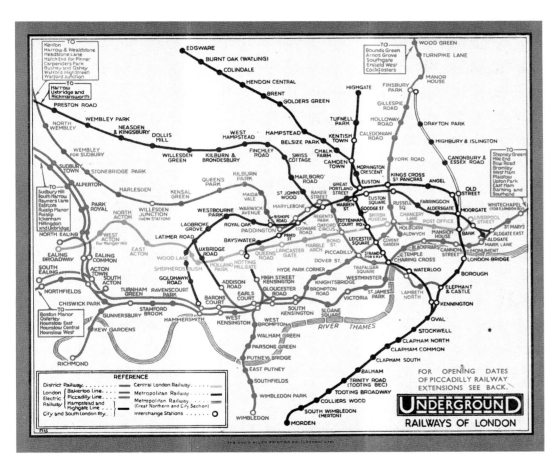

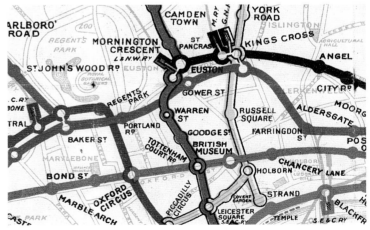

7 Stingemore's last card folder (left), produced in 1932. There was a slight expansion of the central area in comparison with his 1926 version, probably in response to the public's continuing difficulty in deciphering the detail. From April 1926 he had added the line of the River Thames – another concession to the bewildered traveller, perhaps.

8 Detail from 'London Electric Railways' map of c.1909 (above), showing the first use of the 'white-line connector' device for denoting interchange stations. Note, too, the rectangular symbols for main line termini, also linked by white lines to the Underground stations of the same name. Size of whole map 11 x 14¼in (282 x 362mm).

Harry Beck in 1965, holding the exercise book sketch made in 1931.

Photograph: Ken Garland

Chapter 2 The Birth of the Diagram

Henry C Beck (Harry to his friends) was a 29-year-old engineering draughtsman when he produced his first sketch for the Diagram in 1931. At that time he was out of work: a victim, and not for the first time, of the sudden, wholesale sackings that afflicted the public sector and related service industries such as Beck's erstwhile employers, the Underground Group. Ever since 1922, when the government-appointed Commission on National Expenditure chaired by the Tory politician Sir Eric Geddes had first advocated savage economies (the so-called 'Geddes Axe'), Harry Beck and his fellows knew they could be dismissed at short notice, especially if, like him, they were only contracted as temporary employees. In fact, he had been 'temporary'* since his first appointment as a junior draughtsman in the Signal Engineer's office of the Underground Railways in 1925.

Beck's own account of his life at that time, written in 1968 at the request of the present writer, gives an illuminating glimpse of the man himself:

I must have lived a very energetic life in those days. Commuting from Highgate Village, I rarely missed my daily dip in Highgate Pond before breakfast. I became a member of the Signal Office rowing club, rowing behind stroke in a half-outriggered four. I belonged also to the T.O.T. [Train, Omnibus and Tram Staff] Philharmonic Society, to which I was introduced by fellow-draughtsman Fred Webber. But my participation in these social activities had to end because of the temporary nature of my employment.

This was the decade when many a competent artist joined the long and weary queue seeking any work in any department of graphic art. Some months of this, and I consider that I was lucky to be remembered, and recommended for a temporary draughtsman's job, by Ben Lewis, a member of the Philharmonic Society who worked in the Drawing Section of the Establishment Office. I

think that my joy at my recall to the 'old firm' may have sharpened an impish sense of satire, for at home I was mostly to be found doubled up over a drawing board: I kept the staff magazine well supplied with my particular brand of humorous drawing†.

Dismissal again. I was gently told that there was no alternative... the staff of every office had to be pruned, and the last temporary taken on must be sacked.

There follows a passage describing his conception of the Diagram, of which more below. Then:

Lucky for me, pressure of work in the Establishment Office drawing section had built up to such a level that I was invited to return: a letter came offering me further temporary employment, and I was back on the staff a third time.

Bryce Beaumont, who joined the same office as a copywriter in 1936 and who came to be a friend as well as a close colleague, remembered Beck affectionately in a conversation with the writer in 1968. At first, he said, he was in awe at being confronted with the creator of the already renowned Underground Diagram, but was soon more impressed by his benevolence, his pleasing baritone voice and a sense of humour which often relieved the monotony of office work (see Appendix M).

* Temporary staff had fewer rights and less security than 'established' staff. Junior grades could be employed on this basis for many years. The term is not to be confused with the present day temporary worker ('temp' colloquially) usually recruited by an agency and moving from one employer to another as needed.

† Stingemore also indulged in humorous drawings. Perhaps the serious business of map-making and diagramming needed to be balanced by a more frivolous use of their graphic skills.

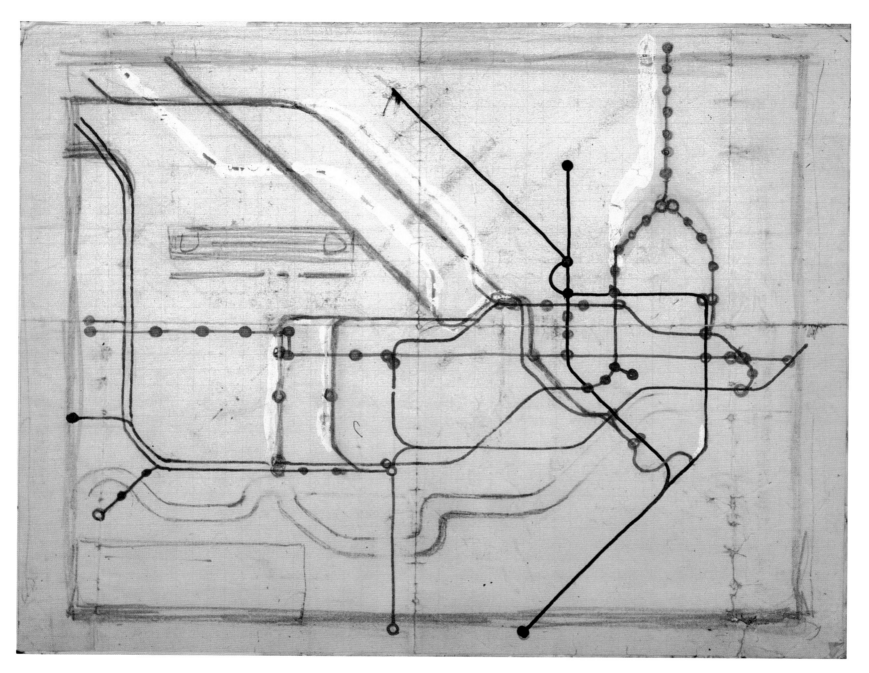

9 Beck's original sketch for the Diagram, made on two pages of an exercise book. Here are the significant features of all the future versions of the design: simplification of the route lines to verticals, horizontals or diagonals; the expansion of the central area; and of course, the elimination of all surface detail except for the line of the River Thames, itself presented in the same stylised form as the route lines.

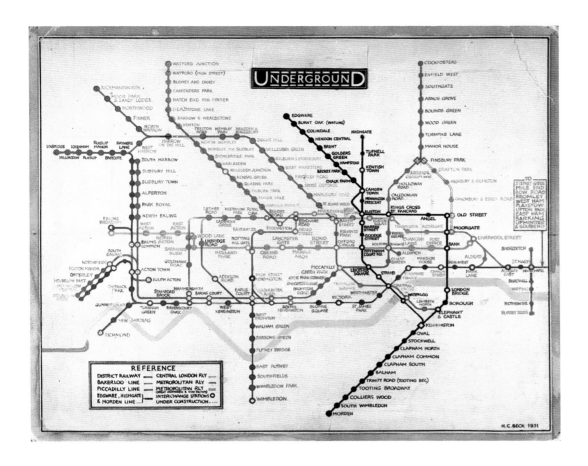

REFERENCE
DISTRICT RAILWAY — CENTRAL LONDON RLY —
BAKERLOO LINE — METROPOLITAN RLY —
PICCADILLY LINE — METROPOLITAN RLY
EDGWARE, HIGHGATE ... INTERCHANGE STATIONS O
& MORDEN LINE ... UNDER CONSTRUCTION ...

H.C. BECK 1931

10 Presentation visual of the Diagram, drawn by Beck to show to the Publicity Department of the Underground. At this stage he was still following the established convention of using blobs to denote stations. The colour coding, too, was the same as that used in the Stingemore maps. It was this visual that was at first rejected in 1931, then accepted the following year as the basis for a trial printing.

How the Underground Diagram was conceived

Beck described his conception of the Diagram thus:

Looking at the old map of the Underground railways, it occurred to me that it might be possible to tidy it up by straightening the lines, experimenting with diagonals and evening out the distance between stations. The more I thought about it the more convinced I became that the idea was worth trying, so, selecting the Central London Railway as my horizontal base line I made a rough sketch. I tried to imagine that I was using a convex lens or mirror, so as to present the central area on a larger scale. This, I thought, would give a needed clarity to interchange information.

From an initial sketch (**9**), made across two facing pages of an exercise book, Beck progressed to a presentation visual (**10**). As his account stated, he had taken the Central London

Railway as a horizontal base line, round which he constructed a network of verticals, horizontals and diagonals. By compressing the outlying portions of the routes he was enabled (a) to include the whole of all routes* except the eastern part of the District Railway beyond Whitechapel; and (b) to enlarge the central portion of the network. At this stage he still employed blobs to denote stations, as in the Stingemore maps, with rings to differentiate interchange stations, though at two of these — Finsbury Park and Kennington — he substituted outline diamonds for rings, possibly for the purpose of demonstrating an alternative to the rings, as these two stations had no special significance that would require such treatment.

Beck showed the design to some colleagues (among them, Stingemore) and they urged him to send it to the Publicity Department. This was in 1931.

Beck's own account continues:

The design was duly submitted, but, to my surprise and disappointment the very idea of a 45- and 90-degree schematic treatment was thought to be too 'revolutionary': my Underground map was handed back to me and that, it seemed, was to be the end of it.

Why did the publicity department dismiss the design so curtly, when it had been so enthusiastically received by Beck's colleagues? Did they fear that, ingenious though it was, it would prove too strange and incomprehensible to the travelling public? If so, it was not the first time, nor would it be the last, that the official mind underestimated the capacity of the public to absorb a new concept.

Though disappointed by rejection, Beck could not let the matter rest:

About a year later [in 1932] *I had another look at the drawing, and decided, without much hope, to try again. This time Mr Patmore of the Publicity Department sent for me, after the Publicity meeting at which it was considered, and greeted me with the words, 'You'd better sit down: I'm going to give you a shock. We're going to print it!' Thus it was, and only, as I believe, through my pertinacity, that the London Underground diagram was born.*

* Though there remains the ambiguity about the westward termination of the Metropolitan Railway, which extended, in some form, as far as Verney Junction until 1936, and as far as Aylesbury until 1961.

The first proof of the Diagram (**11**), in card folder form, was virtually identical to the presentation visual. The only differences of any note were that outline diamonds replaced rings at all interchange stations, that the new branch from Wembley Park to Stanmore was added, and that the Underground Group's black and white logotype — the bar — was now backed by the red ring, the two comprising the bar-and-circle device (often referred to as the bullseye) that had been in increasingly common use on platforms and outside stations since about 1918, though somewhat less commonly on the Underground maps.

In Beck's account of the genesis of the Diagram he makes no mention of the stylized representation of the River Thames, the only surface feature included, and by that token one of the greatest importance. It could be argued that the inclusion of the River Thames was unnecessary and even distracting. However, the travelling public did not think so. (In an informal questionnaire undertaken in 1968 when the writer was preparing the earlier account of the design of the Diagram already referred to, Tube travellers were asked,

among other things, whether or not they found the inclusion of the river on the current diagram to be useful: *without exception* the respondents said they did. Though the questionnaire was not conducted with scientific rigour, the unanimity of response is surely significant.) Given the relative thickness of the river in relation to the route lines, however, it could be said to be too heavy in the first proof; and indeed, it was to be reduced in tone on the printed version.

All the lettering in the first proof — some 440 words — was executed by hand in what Beck described as 'Johnston-style' capitals (see **14**). In fact, Beck took liberties with the letterforms, condensing them as appropriate (compare Tottenham Court Road with Oxford Circus, for example).

In the first printed edition of the Diagram (**12**) the whole thing was redrawn from scratch, with what Beck called 'ticks' replacing the blobs denoting non-interchange stations. This change had three significant advantages: (a) it lightened the Diagram overall, giving it a more elegant appearance; (b) it rectified an imbalance whereby the non-interchange stations appeared bolder than the interchange stations; and (c) each tick pointed unambiguously to the station name to which it referred, so that they could be arranged alternately on different sides of the route lines for greater compactness. There was also an important colour change: the Piccadilly Line was changed from pale blue to dark blue, thus avoiding confusion with the green of the District Railway.

As regards the debut of the Diagram there is some disparity between Beck's account and the documented record. Writing long after the event he said:

Even after the idea was accepted the Publicity Manager was not any too sure about it, and decided to give it a trial run, inviting the travelling public to comment on the new format.

This and a further recollection, given in conversation with the present writer in 1968, that there was a limited initial printing of 'some hundreds', are not borne out by any other evidence. It has been verified that the first edition of the card folder was printed in a quantity of 750,000 and that it was issued in January 1933. If there was, in fact, no trial run, one is left to wonder how the Publicity Manager could have committed the Underground to so vast an initial print order in view of (a) the revolutionary nature of the design, and (b) his own uncertainty about it?

11 Unpublished proof for the first card folder edition, corrected in Beck's own hand. Though he still retained the blobs, he had substituted diamonds for the rings at all interchange stations; and the bar of the Underground logotype was now backed by the red ring to comprise the already familiar 'bullseye' device. All the lettering in this proof was hand drawn by Beck in what he described as 'Johnston-style' capitals. It was a rather loose interpretation – condensed where necessary, as can be seen by comparing Tottenham Court Road with Oxford Circus.

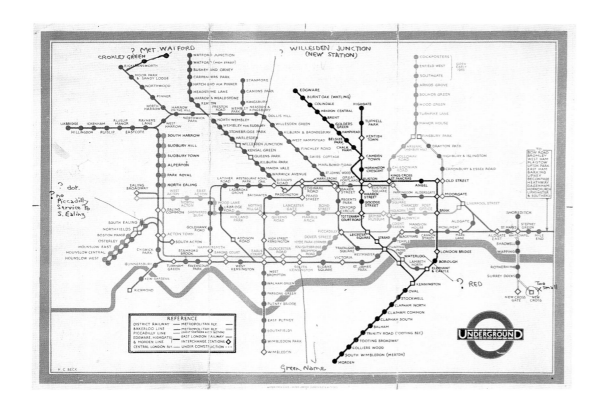

The response of the public to the Diagram

The ordering in January 1933 of 750,000 copies at a cost of £337 10s (equal to about £12,000 at today's prices) was a remarkable turn-around in the official attitude towards the map. That other printings followed soon after – there was one of 100,000 copies in February – is evidence enough that the Diagram was well received by the travelling public.

Why did people take so quickly to this unfamiliar, uncompromising Diagram? The British public is not reputed to welcome innovation, especially in matters visual. Perhaps the answer lies in the fact that it was so obviously useful; people couldn't resist its helpful character, appreciating instinctively that its designer, himself an ordinary, Tube-travelling commuter, was concerned for *their* information needs and not for novelty for its own sake.

Less easy to understand, perhaps, is the great affection in which the Diagram has been held by the public, ever since its first appearance. It might have been expected that the advent of such an abstract, schematised image would generate a response similar to one's first sight of a Mondrian painting; respectful, awed, intrigued, maybe mystified, but surely, never *affectionate*? Yet it was so.

Beck was commissioned to undertake the artwork for a quad royal (40 x 50in/1016 x 1270mm) poster, of which an edition of 2,500 was printed in March 1933 (**13**) and a second edition of 2,000 in August. These were large print orders for posters: a typical print order for the 'artistic' double crown (30 x 20in/762 x 508mm) posters on the Underground at that time was 1,000. Suddenly the Diagram was big business — for the printers of the card folders and the posters, and for the new London Passenger Transport Board which could not have had a better signal for its inauguration as the controlling authority for London's tube, bus, train, tram and trolleybus network on 1 July 1933 — but not for Beck himself, who was paid 5 guineas (£5.25) for the complete poster artwork.

So what had happened was this: in his own time and on his own initiative, an ex-employee of the Underground Railways invented a way to represent London's underground

12 First card folder edition of the Diagram (left) and centre portion of the reverse, folded to form a cover (right), issued in January 1933. The blobs had been replaced by 'ticks' and this simple alteration transformed the design completely, giving it an elegance lacking in the earlier proof. It is difficult to imagine how the increasingly complex versions of the Diagram that were to follow would have succeeded without this small but crucial innovation. Records show that Beck was paid 10 guineas (equal to £380 at today's prices) for the design and artwork. The oft-quoted figure of 5 guineas was the amount paid to him for the quad royal poster artwork.

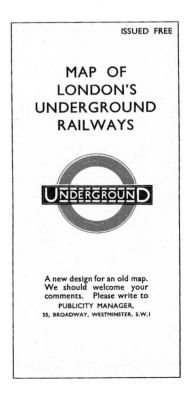

ISSUED FREE

MAP OF
LONDON'S
UNDERGROUND
RAILWAYS

UNDERGROUND

A new design for an old map. We should welcome your comments. Please write to PUBLICITY MANAGER, 55, BROADWAY, WESTMINSTER, S.W.1

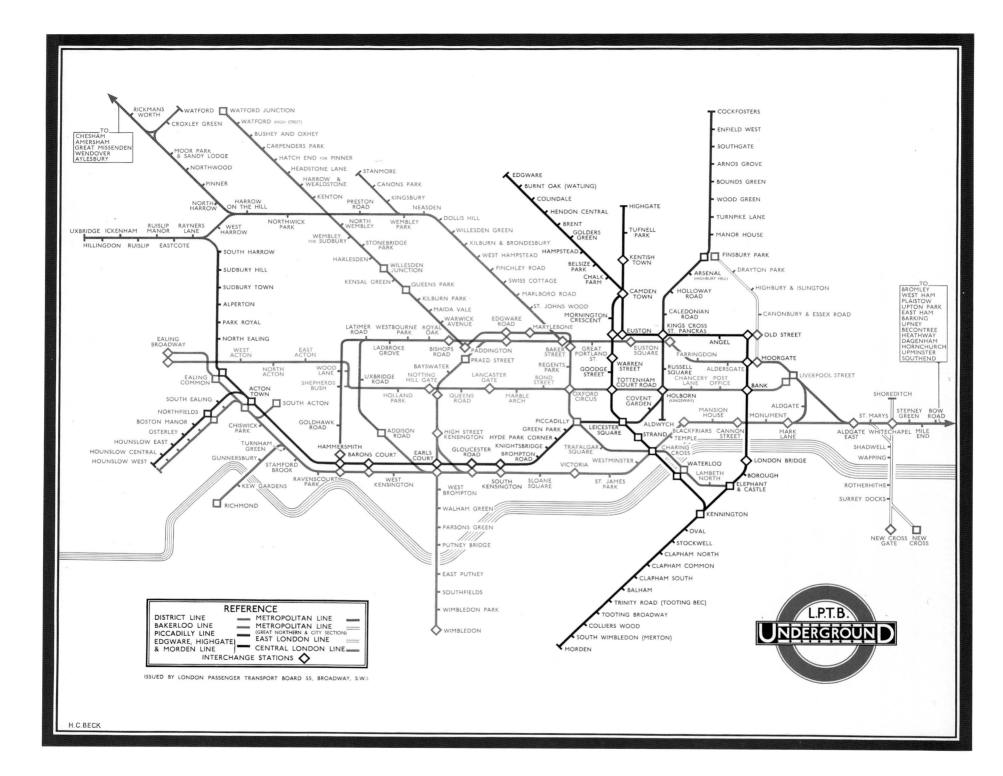

network in diagrammatic form, laying emphasis on its connections rather than its geography; it was flatly rejected by the management; a year later he had another go at them and this time it was cautiously accepted; he was paid a derisory fee; then, although the first card folder edition was printed in substantial quantity, the fact that it contained the request 'A new design for an old map. We should welcome your comments' did not indicate total commitment on the part of London Transport*; the public, however, loved it and suddenly the designer was the blue-eyed boy; his fees, however, remained derisory.

Beck had returned to the employ of the Underground Group in 1932 and was retained on the staff at the inauguration of the London Passenger Transport Board (though he remained a 'temporary' until 1937); so during the artwork, process work, proofing and trial of the card-folder, and then subsequently for the whole of his work on the Diagram, he was both an employee and a contracted freelance. While this situation did, indeed, provide a most valuable insight into the Underground system which no outsider could possibly have gained, it also gave him a problem of status as a designer which dogged his relationship with his client from

the very inception of the Diagram and for the larger part of his working career and after.

Harry Beck married in 1933. Nora Beck could not have known then (neither could her husband) that she had married an obsessive; but he was already fully involved with his invention at the time of their wedding. One wonders if their lives might have been different had she been able to experience at least a couple of years of married life before his — and her — absorption in this totally demanding task. But they were to spend the whole of their married lives under its spell. If Nora had been able to foresee the pain this obsession would bring them in the last years of their marriage, would she have made attempts to steer her spouse away from it, for both their sakes? Perhaps, but the high probability is that it would have made no difference; he was determined to guard and nurture his creation against all opposition.

* In a revealing memo to his Publicity Manager dated 3 August 1933 (that is, long after the Diagram had proved to be a resounding popular success), Frank Pick, Vice Chairman and Chief Executive of the LPTB wrote: 'I had a look at your quad royal map. I confess that upon a large scale this looks very convenient and tidy and is a better map than any we have had so far.' That Pick felt it necessary to 'confess' hints strongly at an earlier lack of enthusiasm; and his phrase 'convenient and tidy' is hardly wholehearted praise for an invention of genius.

13 First quad royal poster of the Diagram, with the imprint '646 . 2000 . 20 3 33' , and the line 'Issued by London Passenger Transport Board' under the reference key. In the few months that had elapsed between the publication of the first card folder in January 1933 and the imprint date on the poster, the design had become a popular success, the first printing of the card folder having been promptly followed by a reprint. The publication of the poster confirmed the primacy of Beck's design as the authoritative representation of the network. Some refinements incorporated since the first card folder edition were: the straightening out of the Bakerloo Line at its northern end, to form a clean diagonal all the way from Paddington to Watford Junction; the 'diagonalisation' of the Stanmore branch of the Metropolitan Line, so avoiding the unhappy rightangle where it diverged from the main

route after Wembley Park; the transferral of Mornington Crescent from the right-hand to the left-hand of the twin lines between Euston and Camden Town, establishing a double-diamond interchange for Euston at the same time; the disappearance of the British Museum station on the Central London Line; the 'diagonalisation' of that portion of the Metropolitan Line between Notting Hill Gate and Edgware Road, avoiding the awkward kink around Paddington; the off-Diagram labelling of the Metropolitan Line beyond Rickmansworth to Aylesbury; and the substitution of more accurate reproductions of Johnston's specially commissioned sans serif type (see **14**) instead of the freely interpreted version Beck had employed on the first card folder. Johnston's letterforms were generously proportioned and the use of capitals only required ample space between the characters. Paradoxi-

cally, this apparently inappropriate edict was to be a key factor in generating a long sequence of designs of rare clarity and distinction. The publication date of the first poster is uncertain: the omission of British Museum station (not closed until 24 September 1933) and the clear indication that the Piccadilly Line was now in operation as far as Cockfosters (opened on 31 July 1933) suggest that the poster was not intended for publication on the imprint date of March but later, perhaps to coincide with the LPTB's inauguration day of 1 July 1933. For many, the first quad royal poster is considered the best of all the many editions executed by Beck over the 27-year period of his stewardship of the Diagram.

ABCDEFG HIJKLMNOPQRS TUVWXYZ

14 Capital letters from Edward Johnston's 'Underground Railways Sans' typeface, used on all versions of the Beck Diagram from the first quad royal poster of March 1933 (lettering for the first card folder of January 1933 having been a somewhat inaccurate, hand-drawn version of this typeface). Although commissioned by Frank Pick, then Commercial Manager of the Underground Group, in 1913, Johnston did not come up with his design until 1916, and it was cut as an exclusive typeface in 1918.

Chapter 3

The System Grows, the Diagram Changes

Although the pattern of the Underground network had been well established by 1933 — there was no completely new Tube line until the opening of the Victoria Line between 1968 and 1971 — some of the existing lines were considerably augmented throughout the next quarter century. Here is a list of the major changes in that period:

Piccadilly Line extended northward from Enfield West (Oakwood) to Cockfosters in July 1933, and westward from South Harrow to Uxbridge in October 1933 (taking over from the District Railway).
Metropolitan Line extended eastward from Whitechapel to Barking in 1936.
Northern Line extended northward from Highgate (now Archway) to East Finchley in 1939.
Bakerloo Line extended northwest from Baker Street as far as Stanmore in 1939 (paralleling the services of the Metropolitan Line to Wembley Park and replacing them to Stanmore).
Northern Line extended northward from East Finchley to High Barnet in 1940 with a branch to Mill Hill East in 1941.
Central Line extended eastward from Liverpool Street to Stratford (taking over from the London & North Eastern Railway) in 1946, to Woodford and Newbury Park in 1947, to Hainault and Loughton in 1948, to Epping and Ongar in 1949 (though not electrified until 1957); also westward from North Acton to Greenford in 1947, and from Greenford to West Ruislip in 1948 over the British Railways ex-Great Western Railway route.

From the above list it can be seen that the designer of the Diagram had to grapple, almost continuously, with the growth and development of the system itself. Indeed, Beck's very first published Diagram of 1933 incorporated a reference to some work under construction (Enfield West to Cockfosters), while the second design — issued a few months later by the LPTB — showed the Metropolitan Railway extending beyond Rickmansworth to Aylesbury, the District Railway branch from Ealing Common transferred to the Piccadilly Line, the renaming of Dover Street station as Green Park, and the proposed closure of British Museum station.

Many designers, it may fairly be supposed, would have regarded each change in the system with some irritation; to be dealt with appropriately, of course, but more as a matter of contractual obligation, or duty, rather than with any sense of eager anticipation. Yet eagerness is exactly what Beck brought to the challenge of every change with which he was presented; partly because, having been an employee, off and on, of the Underground Group since 1925, he was well adjusted to its dynamics; partly because these required modifications to the Diagram would provide him with the opportunity to do some more fine tuning on other aspects of the existing design; and, importantly, because by tackling them with enthusiasm he would be more likely to ensure that the design of the Diagram remained firmly in his own hands. (It may be for this reason that Beck was so amenable to the many suggestions for 'improvements' to the Diagram which were fired at him from the management, including the Board's Chairman, Lord Ashfield, and which were for the most part unhelpful, impractical or even downright fatuous. More of these later.)

In addition to the changes actually effected, there were a number of extensions that received official sanction but which, usually because of shortage of funds, had to be postponed and eventually abandoned. These proposals, too, were frequently required to be shown on the Diagram. Typically, an elaborate development of the Northern Line, extending northwest from Finsbury Park to Alexandra Palace, authorised in 1935, appeared in the Diagram from 1937 to 1941 and again from 1946 to 1950, but was eventually abandoned. These, and several other proposals that never saw the light of day, presented problems every bit as demanding as those that did, to the Diagram's designer.

Even without the special demands arising from proposed extensions, there would be a continuous stream of adjustments and alterations which he was required to implement. A note made by Beck in 1952 (shown at right) sets out a number of these agreed on at a meeting called to discuss the next edition of the Diagram. The nine alterations noted here bear witness to a heavy meeting; all the more so when you notice that they are based on 14 separate drawings submitted by Beck, each one concerned with some aspect of the one edition.

By his own account, Beck appears to have accepted these demands in good part and tackled them promptly:

...these jobs often ran away with all my 'leisure' time for weeks on end. There was the time that I had to forgo sleep for a whole weekend; I was approached on the Friday and asked for a completely finished Diagram, to include some proposed new extensions, and could it be ready by Monday morning, please? It was, and I should mention that during office hours my thoughts were completely concentrated on my Press advertising work, and did we not work until noon on Saturdays then?*

And on the general approach to the dynamics of the problem he writes, with an intriguing choice of metaphor:

Surely the Underground Diagram...must be thought of as a living and changing thing, with schematic and spare-part osteopathy going on all the time.

It is on this assumption that we shall now examine the evolution of the Diagram from its inception to Beck's last version of 1959.

* From 1934 Beck had transferred to the Press Advertising Section of the Publicity Department, where he made layouts, checked proofs, and interviewed artists and writers.

~~At a meeting~~ On 26th January 1952 the Publicity Officer approved the general layout of Drawing No. 7 with the following alterations:

(a) Thicken lines to take names of lines as on current des.
(b) ~~Add~~ grid lines and substitute planer bullseye
(c) Re-arrange section of Piccadilly Line to reduce congestion on District Line (Vic area)
(d) Reduce congestion on Aylesbury section
(e) Reduce congestion on Northern Line (southern ~~section~~ end)
(f) Walham Green: change to Fulham Broadway
(g) River Thames to be named
(h) Draw out suggestions for indicating interchange with Main Line. & new lines.
(i) Move the name Bank

Drawing No. 7 is returned herewith.
As many as possible of the above alterations have been shown on Drawing No 9.
Drawing Nos 10 and 11 show alternative ways of indicating Main Line interchange.
Drawings Nos 12, 13 and 14 show ways of opening out congested areas.

Notes on alterations

(a) ~~This has been done~~: Drg. 9 (Hounslow section) shows treatment.
(b) and (c) alteration carried out on Drg 9.
(d) ~~On Drawing 9~~ The Aylesbury congestion has been slightly reduced, but Drg. 14 shows a ~~much~~ more effective treatment for that area
(e) ~~Drawing 9 has been kept to the standard~~ The design has in the past been reduced without alteration to folder size, and this has fixed the limits of proportion. PTO

15 One of two pages of briefing notes (right) recorded by Beck following a briefing meeting on 26 January in connection with a forthcoming edition of the Diagram.

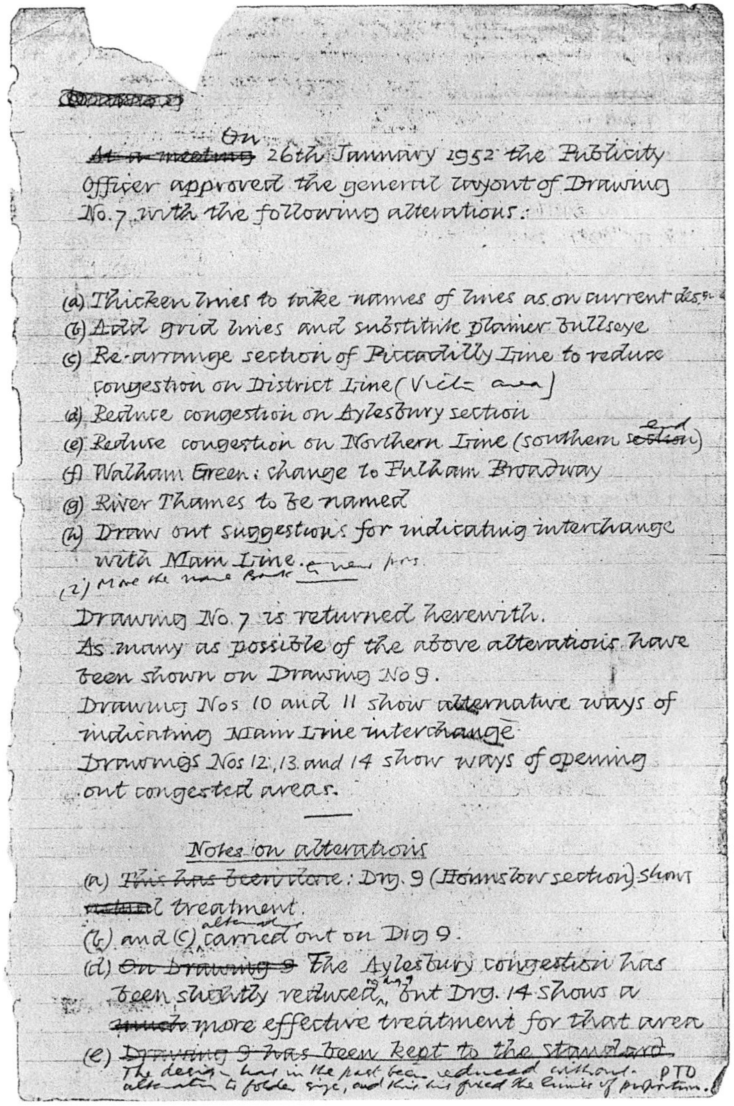

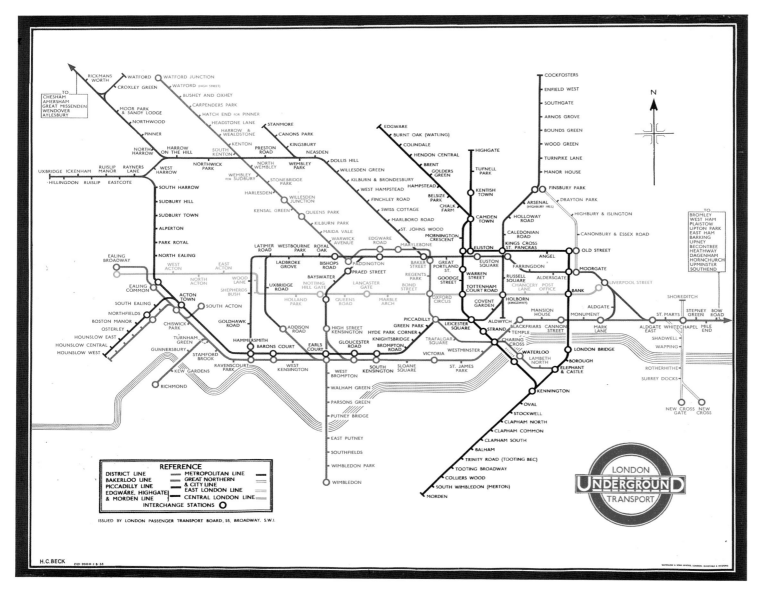

16 Smaller (24 x 30in/610 x 762mm) poster edition, issued August 1933. As well as the modifications already noted on the first quad royal poster, there was one addition – a north pointer – and one alteration – from diamonds to rings for the interchange stations. The intrusive pointer, a singularly inappropriate device, would disappear within short order but the rings were to become the preferred symbols for this purpose (though not exclusively so).

17 Spoof diagram by Beck (right), forming a whole page (turned on its side for this purpose) of the *Train, Omnibus and Tram Staff Magazine* for March 1933, using electrical references in place of the station names; a clear hint at one of the sources of inspiration for the Diagram itself.

Chapter 4 Refinement, Experiment and Consistency

A strong claim can be made for the proposition that the quad royal poster version of the Diagram dated March 1933 is the classic version: refined, harmonious, excellent of its kind. Certainly, it is all of these; and it has, in addition a quality of elegance that lifts it above the category of sound information design into something with a wider, more general significance.

Although this was only the first poster version of the Diagram, the design had improved considerably since the presentation visual of 1931. The use of blobs to denote stations, retained in the first, experimental proof of the card folder, had been rejected in favour of 'ticks' for the first

published edition; diamonds had been chosen as the most suitable way of showing the interchange stations; and the hand-drawn lettering of the card folder edition had been replaced by accurate reproductions of Johnston's Underground Railways Sans type (**14**). Simply because there was more room, a more delicate balance of weight between route lines and lettering was possible in a large poster format.

The second edition of the poster (**16**), dated August 1933, though very similar to the first, had an unhappy and in-appropriate intrusion: a north pointer. This was added by some busybody who had no appreciation of the difference between a map representing geographical reality and a purely geometric, straight line diagram representing connections. Beck was not informed, let alone consulted, before its inclusion, and contrived stealthily to remove it at the earliest opportunity. Another change was the substitution of rings for diamonds to denote interchange stations. While it is un-deniable that diamonds proved to be less convenient than circles for the purpose, there was, it can be argued, a special character about the former that lent this version of the Diagram a rare, perhaps unique, distinction.

An electrical allusion

At this point it seems appropriate to refer to a whimsical diversion (**17**) perpetrated by Beck in the *Train, Omnibus and Tram Staff Magazine* (published as the *T.O.T. Magazine*) for March 1933. In answer to those of his colleagues who ribbed him that he had merely adapted one of the electrical circuits with which he was so familiar in his work, and imposed it on the Underground map, he came up with a version in which station names were replaced by electrical references. The thing was strewn with bad puns ('Bakerlite Tube' for Bakerloo Line, 'Amp' for Hampstead) and sly allusions to

THE UNDERGROUND "STRAIGHT EIGHT" ALL-ELECTRIC SKIT-SET CIRCUIT DIAGRAM

SPECIFICATION
London Regional Stations, connecting H.T. Output Cells with Ohms. Bare copper inductance with minimum or no Resistance.

H.C. BECK. A.E.Inst.O.U.

18 Third card folder edition, c.September 1933. Similar to the second edition except for (a) the smoothing out of a kink in the District Line between Ealing Common and Ealing Broadway, left over when the outward stretch from Ealing Broadway was handed over to the Piccadilly Line; (b) the substitution of 'London Transport' for 'L.P.T.B.' within the bullseye; and (c) the inclusion of the new escalator connection between Bank and Monument stations, accompanied by an ostentatious notice to this effect. Though the notice became progressively less prominent in time, the devices used to denote this feature were to absorb the attentions of the designer out of all proportion to its importance (see p 49). The substitution of accurate reproductions of Johnston's 'Underground Railways Sans' typeface (see **14**) in place of Beck's more flexible version, while presenting no difficulty on the posters, was to present the designer with endless problems of fitting station names into the limited space available on the card folder format.

national institutions in the locality of the station ('Cabinet and C.I.D. Lightning Arresters' substituted for Westminster). It is interesting that in his own account of the genesis of the Diagram, Beck did not mention the electrical circuit diagrams which must, surely, have been a major inspiration for his concept; and that this jokey aside was the only reference he made, then or later, while commentators rarely miss an opportunity to draw the parallel.

Colour coding

The colour coding of the tube lines was a matter for much discussion at this time. There was a tendency for the public to confuse the orange of the Central London Line with the red of the Bakerloo Line. In addition, Beck realised that the orange was tonally weak, and instead of the Central Line appearing as the strong, horizontal base line he had intended, it was somewhat overpowered by the other lines. By 1934* the Central became red, with the incidental benefit that the station names were seen much more legibly against the white background than when they were orange; the Bakerloo Line was changed to brown (**19**). Whether at Beck's instigation or by another agency, this was a considerable improvement. However the possibility of confusion caused the management, as we shall see later, to find an additional method of distinguishing one line from another.

It may be helpful here to touch upon colour coding and colour discrimination, a subject on which there was only the slimmest literature in the mid-thirties. There was one factor, however, which even a lay person could have observed: that colour discrimination is likely to be less easy when lighting conditions are poor. While the lighting was good inside the stations and on the platforms, it varied greatly in the streets outside the stations, where the Diagram posters were also displayed. As to colour blindness: opticians and physiologists already knew that red-green confusion was not uncommon, especially in men, and that green-blue confusion, though not as common, was not insignificant. But this expert

* First seen on card folder No 2 of that year.

26

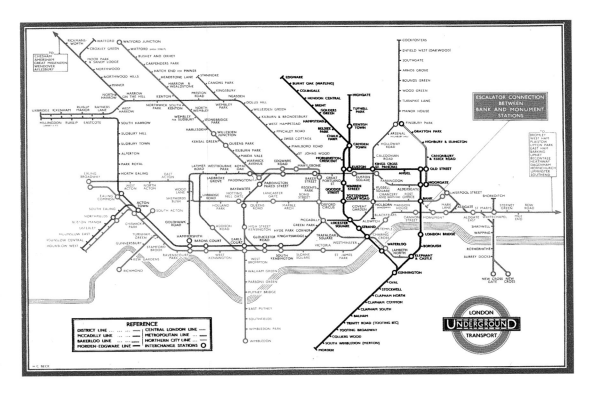

19 Card folder edition No 2 1934. In this design, the problem of confusion between the Central London Line and the Bakerloo Line, caused by their respective colours of orange and red, was resolved by changing the Central London Line to red and the Bakerloo Line to brown: a marked improvement that has been retained ever since. There were other changes: the Piccadilly Line was now shown extending from South Harrow to Uxbridge, running alongside the Metropolitan Line; the East London Line was absorbed into the Metropolitan, the route colour consequently altering from a red outline to purple; and the right-hand curve on the Watford branch line where it joined the Metropolitan's main route to Rickmansworth and Aylesbury was omitted, the westward service from the Watford branch having been discontinued on the last day of 1933. The service returned afterwards but was never shown again on the Diagram

information*, though available, was not sought by those responsible for devising colour codes (and is quite likely not to be sought, even today). In view of the unscientific, *ad hoc* approach by Beck and his clients, it is noteworthy that, with relatively minor adjustments, the colours of the route lines have remained the same ever since, even to the extent of being able to accommodate two new lines — Victoria and Jubilee — requiring two more colours, and also the more recent identities given to the Hammersmith & City and East London Lines.

Some 'improvements'

The Diagram was altogether a most tempting object for the management to get their hands on; so they did. Fortunately, all their 'suggestions' for 'improvements', many of which were instructions to incorporate pointless or distracting variations, were, with rare exceptions, implemented through Beck himself. Because of this he never lost control of the essence of the design, and was able to get it back on course

each time the 'improvement' was shown to be not so. In some cases, he recorded, there were:

... the inevitable ideas for 'improvements' that had to be tactfully repulsed... amongst them was one from Lord Ashfield [Chairman of the LPTB], *who wanted to see a central-area diagram with all interchange station names set out in 'bullseye'* [that is, bar-and-circle device] *panels as they appear on the stations, but the idea rather defeated itself: for legibility, the panels had to be so large that they interfered with continuity.*

Presumably Beck was able to dissuade Ashfield from so harebrained a notion by means of a sketch demonstrating its impracticality†. In other cases, though, he had to go a lot

* For a reasonably up-to-date summary of scientific thinking on colour discrimination and colour blindness, see Gregory, R L, *Eye and Brain*, Weidenfeld & Nicolson, London 1990.

† Ashfield would already have seen one unsatisfactory map of the Underground incorporating such a device: an ingenious concoction designed by A L Gwynne and published in January 1933 (see Appendix A).

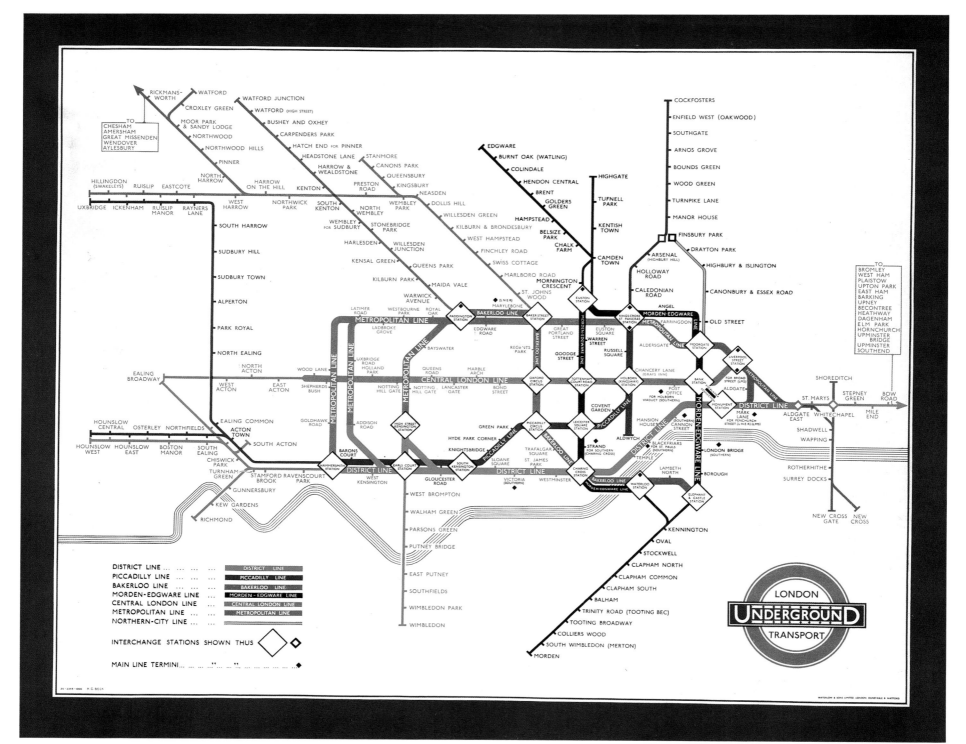

20 Quad royal poster of 1935 (left). A most peculiar aberration, incorporating two features imposed on Beck by the Board, which gave Beck a great deal of trouble and no satisfaction at all: the thickening of the lines in the central area so as to include the route names within them in white; and the use of large, white diamonds for the central interchanges with the station names inside them – and not only the names but also the word 'Station' and, for the main line termini, a little black diamond as well. Thus the central area, cluttered with thickened lines and outsized diamonds, was imposed on an otherwise virtually unchanged Diagram. Beck undertook the line thickening with little enthusiasm; the outsized diamonds were anathema to him. He remembered thinking at the time that such a bizarre notion could not survive more than one edition. Alas, it was not so. The colour coding on this edition is also a matter for some concern. Unaccountably, the colour of the Metropolitan Line was changed from purple to a deep red hardly distinguishable from the vermilion of the Central London Line. This proved so obviously unsatisfactory that it would be promptly changed; but not entirely for the better.

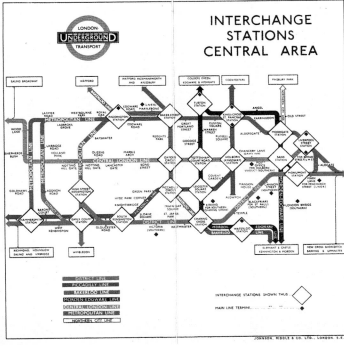

21 Reverse of a 1935 card folder edition of the Diagram, containing a representation of the central area of the network with the interchange station names inside large diamonds, as on the quad royal poster of the same year (the smaller scale preventing its incorporation on the Diagram proper).

further than that. In 1935 (**20**) the use of diamonds for the interchange stations was revived, but in a particularly dire form: 20 of the most central interchanges were denoted by large outline diamonds with the names of the stations printed inside them: an absolute nonsense, since the lettering had to be so small, in order to accommodate such names as Tottenham Court Road Station (yes, they even insisted that the word 'station' be included as well!) that it was appreciably smaller than the lettering of all other stations. Beck totally disapproved of the idea but he loyally incorporated it in the new quad royal poster. On this same design:

I was told to thicken the route lines so that the name of each, e.g. Northern Line, could appear in white capitals within its thickness.

These two features — the outsized diamonds and the thickened route lines — had the effect of altering the Diagram markedly for the worse. Beck hoped this version would be seen right away for the aberration it was; but he was compelled to put up with outsized diamonds until 1937, by which year the thickened route lines had been extended over the whole Diagram (**22**) — though not so thick as in the 1935 version.

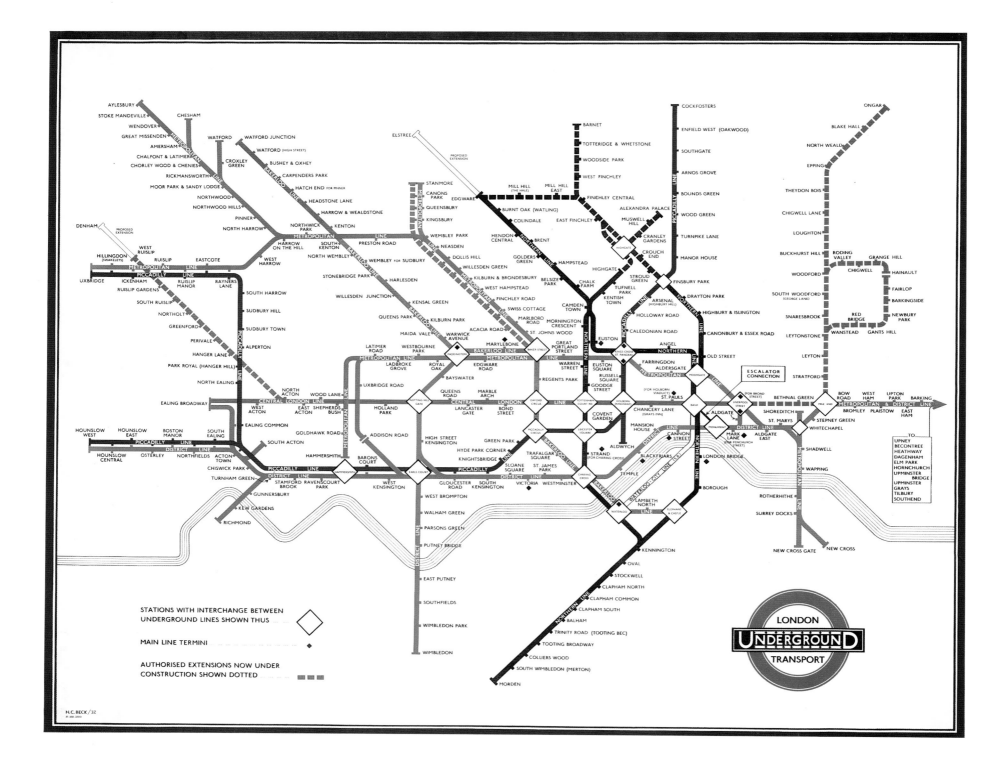

STATIONS WITH INTERCHANGE BETWEEN
UNDERGROUND LINES SHOWN THUS

MAIN LINE TERMINI

AUTHORISED EXTENSIONS NOW UNDER
CONSTRUCTION SHOWN DOTTED

LONDON
UNDERGROUND
TRANSPORT

H.C. BECK /32

30

For obvious reasons of scale, the device of enlarged diamonds with station names inside them was not used on the overall Diagram in the card folder editions, but it was employed, with fair success, in the accompanying representation of the central area on the reverse of the folder (**21**). Though this use of the device was discontinued when it was abandoned on quad royal editions, it reappeared in similar form on card folders between 1949 and 1954, with the diamonds replaced by rings.

A second quad royal of 1937 disposed of the mistaken concept of putting the station name inside the diamonds, allowing Beck to reduce the latter in size — though they remained prominent — and to restore the names themselves to the same size as all the other stations.

Two quad royal versions of 1937 were required to display information which transformed them from their predecessors; they included for the first time a proposed, vast extension of the Central London Line, to the east and northeast as far as Ongar, and to the northwest as far as Ruislip (or

Denham in the case of the smaller-diamond version). Shown in broken lines, the extensions were described in the attached keys as 'authorised extensions'. The two branches designated to terminate at Hainault, one via Redbridge (at that time spelt Red Bridge), the other via Chigwell, formed a virtual loop: a feature quite unlike any other on the Diagram so far, and one that provided a welcome touch of the unexpected in the top right hand corner of the design.

As to thickening the route lines in order to insert the route names in white within them, this was dropped in the late 1930s, but then revived from 1946 until Beck's last design in 1959. Though he was not happy with it the first time round he appears to have returned to it with rather more equanimity.

A profitless experiment

The proposed extension of the Central London Line (renamed the Central Line in late 1937) to east and west was one of the factors that led Beck to undertake a vast speculative work (see Appendix B):

In 1938... I spent a long time building up a comprehensive diagram of the whole rail system of Greater London... this colossal piece of homework earned me nothing: I was told there was too much on it.

One is tempted to ask why, on the evidence of the first edition of the Diagram in 1933 — received with such unexpected delight by the travelling public — London Transport could not bring itself at least to issue a trial printing of this experimental design. It is possible the public might have agreed with the management of LT that 'there was too much on it' for their liking; they were never given the chance to find out*. But even if LT was justified in not giving the comprehensive diagram wide publication, could it not have printed a limited edition for internal use? After all, this was a unique visualisation of what was probably the most intricate pattern of rail connections in the world. Even if it was 'too much' for the public, it was surely not too much for the experts?

22 Quad royal poster of 1937. The thickened lines, first seen in the 1935 poster, were still in evidence, though somewhat less thick and now extended over the whole Diagram. The diamonds, too, were still there, though reduced in size and no longer burdened with the redundant word 'Station' inside them. The Metropolitan Line was no longer coloured deep red, so avoiding the confusion present in the 1935 poster, but had become a green identical with the District Line. No doubt there was some internal logic that had governed this, possibly connected with ideas that were being discussed at the time for greater interworking between the two 'surface' lines. But to the outside observer – and most particularly in the eyes of the ordinary traveller – it was surely puzzling: why were two otherwise distinct Underground lines now sharing a common route colour? But puzzling or not, this coding scheme was to persist until 1949, when the Metropolitan Line reverted to its previous purple identification. Another, less puzzling, change in colour was that the station names, until then in self-colours (that is, in the same colours as the route lines themselves) were now all in black. It had the effect of changing the balance of weight between the route lines and the lettering, not for the better, and removed a most distinctive feature of the Diagram. On the other hand, it went some way to overcoming an imbalance whereby the Northern Line had appeared doubly dominant – having a black route line and black lettering in contrast to, say, the green of the District Line and did away with the need to repeat station names where more than one line was involved. With this edition of the Diagram, Beck was charged with a new requirement of introducing the proposals of the 'New Works Programme 1935-40' which had been announced by London Transport in June 1935. He had to show a complex of northward extensions of the Northern Line and two lengthy extensions eastward and westward on the Central London Line (soon to be renamed the Central Line). The inclusion of the proposed extensions (by broken lines) constituted one of the greatest challenges to Beck as designer. It was a matter of no small regret to him that he was tackling it at the same time as he was compelled to deal with the footling nonsense of the outsized diamond interchange symbols. But at least, in this case as in all editions of the Diagram since its inception, he was the responsible designer; the following year was to offer a quite different challenge, this time to his own stewardship.

* Until 1973, that is, when the 'London's Railways' diagram appeared (see Appendix L).

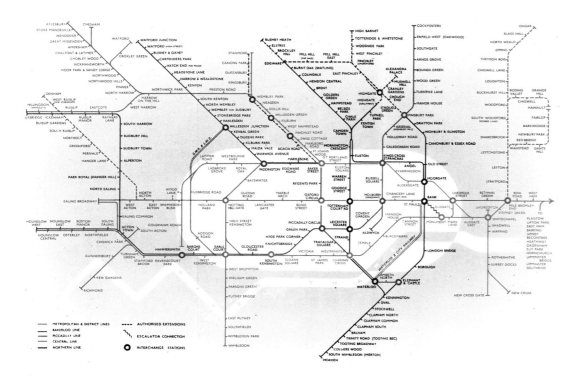

23 Card folder of 1938. A version of Beck's design executed by another hand without his foreknowledge. An airbrush technique was used to emphasise the central area and to indicate the line of the river (the latter counterchanging in tone where it entered the central area); the route lines were more slender than in any previous version of the Diagram; interchange stations denoted by single bold rings; and appreciably more space was gained for the design by removing the heavy border used on all previous card folders. With the exception of the last, all these changes were for the worse. The fact that this version was done by a designer of considerable ability, yet was a poor thing in comparison with Beck's original, demonstrates all the more clearly how well attuned the latter was to the demands of the Diagram. Note that the station names in this version are self-coloured, not black as in Beck's quad royal of 1937.

24 A quad royal poster of 1940 (right). Beck was confronted with three new requirements from the Board: to use interlinked rings for the interchange stations; to duplicate a large number of station names on the grounds that they served two Underground lines; and to change the 45° diagonals to 60° diagonals, on the supposition that this would accommodate more easily the (proposed) northeastward extension of the Central Line. The interlinked rings (mostly pairs but with some triplets) were clumsy and unhelpful; the duplication of the station names was a great irritation to Beck, included at the insistence of the Operating Department, but he was to be stuck with them until 1946; the 60° lines were not the boon they might at first have appeared to be, and were dropped.

Enter another hand

In this same year Beck was confronted by a serious challenge to his stewardship of the Diagram: a card folder version (**23**) closely based on his own design, but by another hand* (though unsigned). The interchange rings had been emboldened and the route lines had been made more slender; but the most distinctive modification was the addition of an airbrush rendering in blue-green, intended to highlight the central area. This was an irrelevance and an obfuscation. Where the graduated tone was at its strongest it reduced the legibility of some station names, especially those on the Metropolitan and District Lines, printed in green.

Beck was appalled at the result. In a letter to Christian Barman, the Publicity Officer of London Transport, dated 2 June 1938, he wrote:

I have just happened to see a proof of a new Underground folder. The 'H.C. Beck' diagram has been used, but with considerable and, I suggest, undesirable, alterations by another artist — one not on the staff — without reference to me.

The idea of redesigning the old geographical Underground map in diagram form was conceived by me in 1931; the original diagram, published in 1932 [sic] was of my own invention and design. Every variation in it since has been either made by me or made by the lithographer under my supervision.

When I recently signed a form assigning the copyright of this design to the Board, it was not merely understood, but was promised, that I should continue to make, or edit and direct, any alterations that might have to be made to the design. This practice has been followed without exception since 1932.

I wish therefore to place on record my protest against the action taken in the present instance.

Barman replied in a memorandum dated June 8, 1938:

Thank you for your note of June 2. I agree with you that this diagram has been altered and not altogether for the better. An artist

* It has recently been established beyond doubt that this was Hans Schleger who, under the pseudonym Zero, had already designed a number of distinguished promotional posters for London Transport.

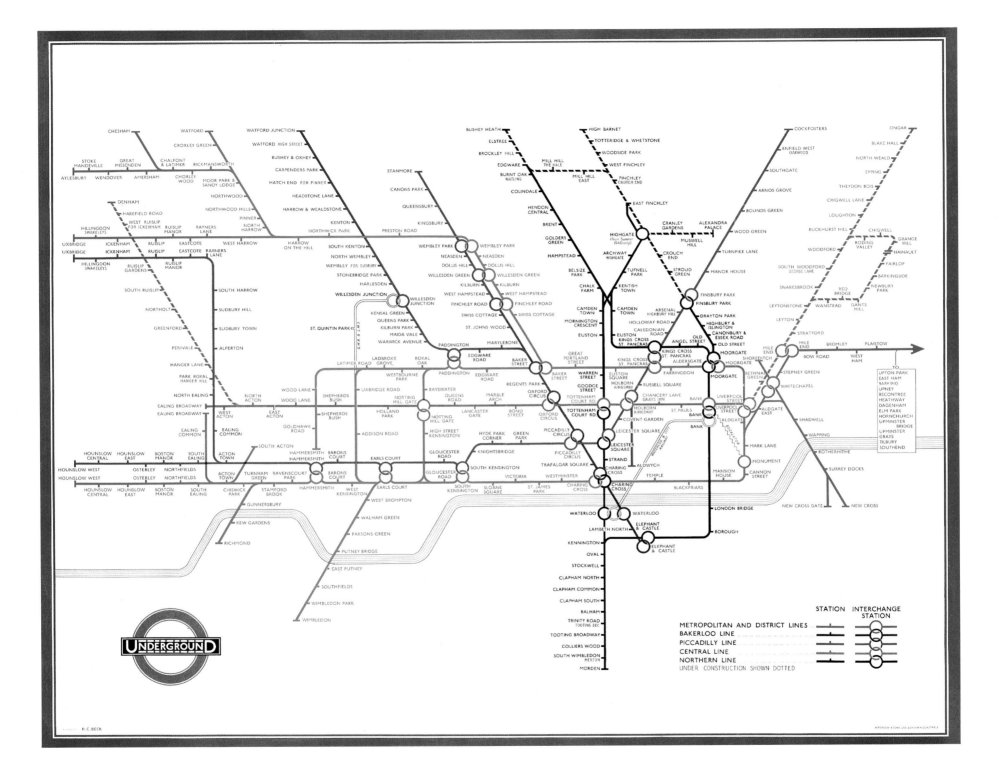

UNDERGROUND

was engaged with the one object of trying by means of a coloured background and a different station indication to emphasise the inter-change facilities of the Underground so that the special (and I think very ugly) inter-change map might be dispensed with. Neither Mr. Patmore nor myself quite realised how far he had gone before we saw a proof. I hope you will make a note of your points and let Mr. Patmore have them so that the diagram may be put right when next reprinted.

Beck was naturally relieved to have Barman's confirmation of his own poor view of the altered diagram. He was not so reassured to note that nothing was said in Barman's memo regarding the promise about his (Beck's) continuing responsibility for the Diagram. That issue was to resurface in 1946 and again in 1960 when, as we shall see, he was to become embroiled in a bitter dispute which caused him immense distress. For the time being, however, his forthright defence of his position had the desired effect, and he was duly consulted on, and made responsible for, all design changes.

The episode of the linked rings and other oddities

In 1939 Beck set about incorporating three new devices in one Diagram (**24**), issued in early 1940: the use of pairs and triplets of interlinked rings to denote interchange stations; the duplication of a large number of station names serving two lines and the triplication of four of them; and a change in the angle of diagonal route lines from 45° to 60° to the horizontal. While some justification could be advanced for the latter, on the basis that it could more conveniently encompass the proposed Central Line extensions to the northeast and northwest, the use of multiple rings as interchange station symbols merely added complexity without increasing

clarity; on the duplication of station names, Beck knew this to be a pointless exercise at the outset ('I was not happy about it', he wrote later) but he carefully tried to meet the wishes of the Operating Department, which had a bee in its bonnet about the matter. The interlinked rings and the 60° angle did not last beyond 1941, but the unhappy and unnecessary duplication and triplication of station names were to remain a feature of the Diagram until 1946.

The three changes listed above were imposed on Beck by others, but one other unsatisfactory feature of the 1939 version cannot be blamed on anyone else: the wide separation of Wimbledon station on the District Line from South Wimbledon on the Northern Line. Since the two lines are quite close to each other at this point, the divergence on the Diagram was misconceived and puzzling.

Going rectangular

During 1940, and with the encouragement of Christian Barman (who remained Publicity Officer until 1941), Beck worked on a considerably revised design for the Diagram (**25**) which entailed reducing the diagonals to an absolute minimum. First published in January 1941, this version undoubtedly raised a few eyebrows at London Transport. The Diagram had now moved a long step further from on-the-ground, geographical reality. For Beck it was another stage in his search for simplicity and clarity (though he was still saddled, to his annoyance, with the duplication and triplication of many of the station names); to others, perhaps, it was a stage too far. But whatever reservations there might have been, they did not have any effect on the design from that time until Beck's last version of 1959: all Underground Diagrams during this period remained rectilinear in form.

25 A quad royal poster of 1941 (opposite). A much altered configuration, in which Beck reduced the diagonals to a minimum, and which set the style for the Diagram right up to Beck's last version of 1959. He was still very hampered by the duplication and triplication of many station names which had been imposed on him the previous year, and the District and Metropolitan Lines were still sharing the same route colour, against his better judgement; but still in other respects he seemed to have had his own way in progressing to an even more abstract form, in the belief that it would provide even greater clarity of information. Beginning with this version, and until 1946, all proposed extensions were omitted from the Diagram.

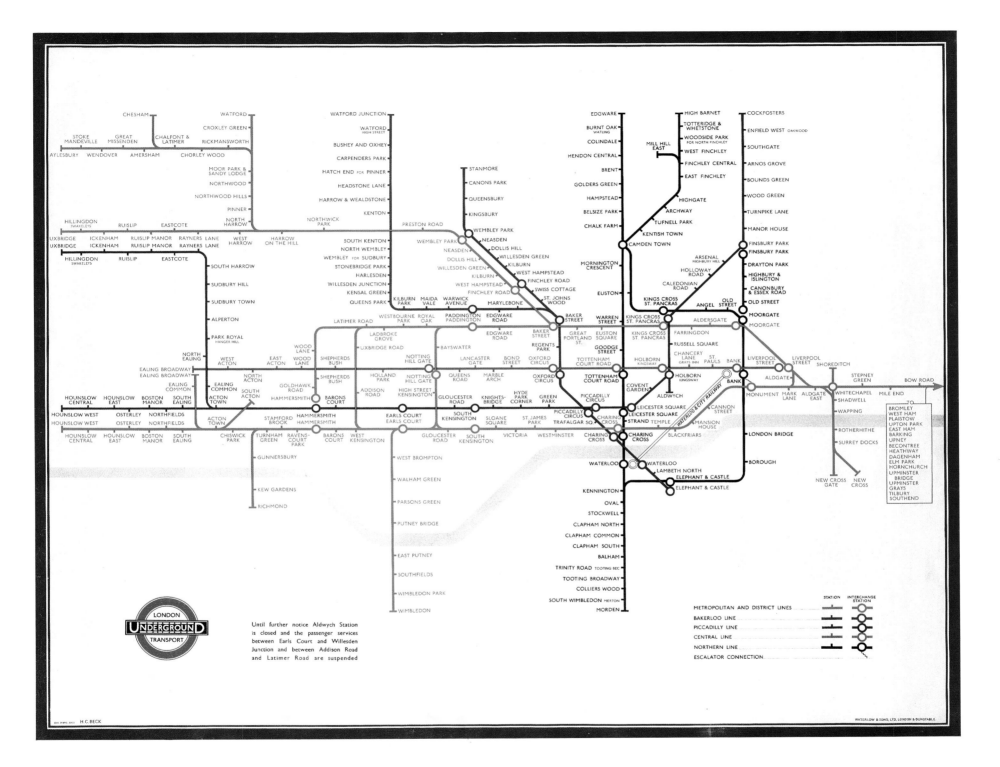

Until further notice Aldwych Station is closed and the passenger services between Earls Court and Willesden Junction and between Addison Road and Latimer Road are suspended

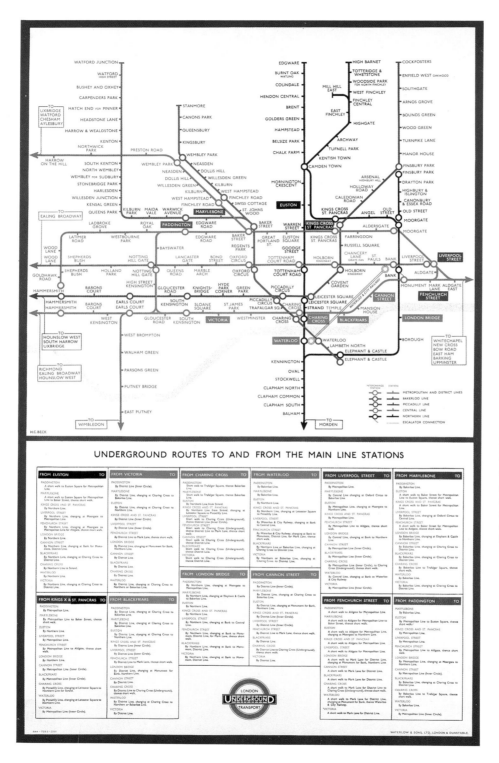

26 A double royal poster of 1944. Although the quad royal posters were the normal format for the general display of the Diagram, other formats were often employed, as in this instance, where the Diagram was used to show Underground routes to and from the main line stations. Here Beck adapted the design to fit a square space at the top of the poster, allowing a lesser space below for specific information in tabular form, linked to the Diagram by coloured rectangles with the main line stations in white lettering inside them. The northern extremities of the lines are shown on the Diagram but those terminating to the east, west and south are not shown in full. One would have thought that, in theory, the use of a colour code for these rectangles would conflict with the colour coding of the tube lines, but it appears not to be so, though only a user test could confirm this. An effective demonstration by Beck of the Diagram's flexibility.

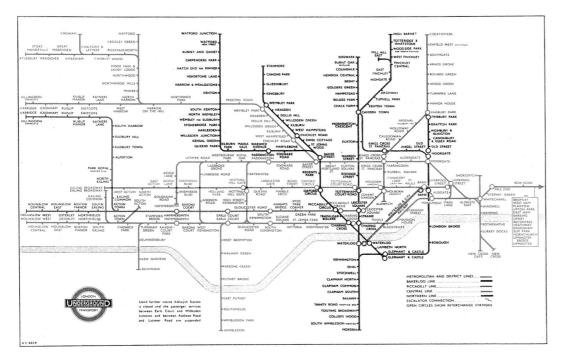

27 Card folder No 1 1945, showing (a) how little the design changed since 1941, and (b) the fine adjustments necessary to accommodate the station names in the card folders as compared with the quad royal posters, 23. In the former category only one design change has been spotted: the Metropolitan Line branch terminating at Hammersmith rated an interchange ring in 1941 whereas from 1943 it had been relegated to a terminal 'tick' (but note that by 1946, 28, it had once again become an interchange station). The showing of interchanges at places where stations are not adjacent caused much debate within the organisation over the years. There were many minor adjustments to the positioning of station names; for example, in the card folder the station names Gloucester Road, Leicester Square and Monument had to straddle route lines – always a matter of regret to Beck since it broke the flow he was so keen to preserve – whereas this was not necessary in the quad royal posters. There were also a number of re-groupings of interchange stations (note especially Charing Cross), presumably also because of the difficulty of squeezing duplicated and triplicated station names into so small a compass.

The proposed extensions of the Central and Northern Lines were delayed during the war years, and were not shown on the wartime Diagrams after 1941 (27). This was the most stable period in its evolution. The Central Line now formed a true axis as a straight horizontal running from Ealing Broadway in the west to Liverpool Street in the east.

1946 brought back the proposed extensions (28). These had to be incorporated within the rectilinear Diagram for the first time, providing Beck with a welcome challenge. At the same time, to his great joy, he was allowed to get rid of the nonsensical duplication and triplication of station names which had bedevilled the Diagram since the fateful version of 1939. Most significantly, the 'white-line connector' referred to earlier (see p 13), first seen in a map dated 1909, was reintroduced with great effect to denote all interchange stations (29). Beck's use of this device was so assured that, in effect, he made it his own; certainly, it was never better employed than it was by him.

There was a confidence in his handling of the Diagram during this period that suggests Beck was being given a relatively free hand; but we have two pieces of evidence which indicate this was not so. One is a copy of a memo from him to H T Carr, Acting Publicity Officer, dated 3rd July 1946:

May I draw attention to the fact that alterations have been made to the underground diagram map without reference to me.

When at a meeting in November 1937 I agreed to transfer the copyright of the design to London Transport it was promised as a condition that all alterations were to be made or edited by me, and that I was to be given a fee and treated as an outside artist.

In June, 1938 I had occasion to protest that this condition was not being observed... but since that time, as far as I am aware, I have had no reason to complain, except in the case of maps now exhibited or in preparation.

We cannot know at this remove what 'alterations' were being referred to in the memo. However, there is another piece of evidence that demonstrates an effort by others to add their two-pennorth: a quad royal poster (**29**) dated August 1946 which has been garnished with a gaudy border and a decorative heading. Though Beck's name was still in the bottom left-hand corner, he had to share a credit with 'Shep', whose name appeared on the right-hand corner of the border itself. While not intended to do so, the effect of this ostentatious border was to upstage the Diagram itself. But, though irritating, it was unlikely to have been the cause of Beck's complaint. After some prodding, he had the following response from Carr, in a memo dated 12th July, 1946:

Underground Beck Diagram

Confirming interview this afternoon, as mentioned, I shall be only too pleased to consider any improvements which may occur to you from time to time in connection with the diagrammatic map we *now have exhibited on our stations, and should they be accepted pay you an adequate sum.*

Further, it is understood that if you, in your own time, can carry out any alterations which we desire, such work shall be paid for at commercial rates.

As with the earlier exchange of memos with Christian Barman in 1938, there is a notable caginess in regard to Beck's claim that he had a promise that 'all alterations were to be made or edited by me'. There is no acknowledgement of the validity of the promise, nor any guarantee that Beck would be solely responsible for future versions of the Diagram. At the time, he would probably have been no more than mildly annoyed at this omission. If he saw a potential problem it would have appeared as a cloud no bigger than a man's hand.

A new device appeared in 1947 (**30**), though it represented a long-established feature of the system itself: a distinctive outlining of the Inner Circle — not a separate line but part of

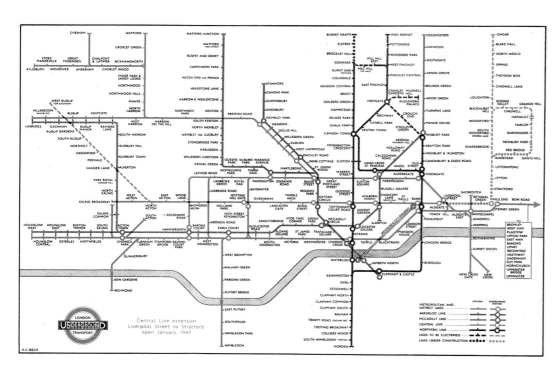

28 Card folder of January 1946. There were three significant changes: the abandonment of self-colours for the station names in favour of black printing (previously introduced for the quad royal poster of 1937 but not on card folders); the abolition of the futile and disruptive practice of duplicating and triplicating many station names; and the restoration of 'Lines to be electrified' and 'Lines under construction' on the Central and Northern Lines, indicated by broken lines and dotted lines respectively.

29 Quad royal poster of August 1946 (right). Both poster and folder of the same year are shown here for comparison. Note that (a) the poster used thickened lines to enable the inclusion of route names within them, a device not feasible in the card folder; (b) uniquely, a garish, inappropriate border had been drawn by the designer Captain Shepherd and signed with his pen-name 'Shep' in the bottom righthand corner, to balance Beck's own signature in its usual place in the bottom lefthand corner; (c) there was one more step in the 'rectification' process, whereby the parallel stretch of the Metropolitan and Bakerloo Lines from Baker Street to Wembley Park, a diagonal in the card folder, became a vertical in the poster; and (d) Beck introduced, to great effect, the 'white-line connector' for interchange stations, borrowed from some Underground maps of 1909-12 (see p 13) but never better used than in this revival.

LONDON'S UNDERGROUND

CHESHAM · WATFORD · CROXLEY GREEN · STOKE MANDEVILLE · GREAT MISSENDEN · CHALFONT & LATIMER · RICKMANSWORTH · AYLESBURY · WENDOVER · AMERSHAM · CHORLEY WOOD

WATFORD JUNCTION · WATFORD HIGH STREET · BUSHEY AND OXHEY · CARPENDERS PARK · HATCH END for PINNER · HEADSTONE LANE · HARROW & WEALDSTONE · NORTHWICK PARK · KENTON

MOOR PARK & SANDY LODGE · NORTHWOOD · NORTHWOOD HILLS · PINNER · NORTH HARROW

WEST RUISLIP for ICKENHAM · HILLINGDON SWAKELEYS · RUISLIP · EASTCOTE · UXBRIDGE · ICKENHAM · RUISLIP MANOR · RAYNERS LANE · RUISLIP GARDENS · SOUTH RUISLIP · NORTHOLT · GREENFORD · PERIVALE · HANGER LANE · PARK ROYAL HANGER HILL · NORTH EALING · WEST HARROW · HARROW ON THE HILL · SOUTH HARROW · SUDBURY HILL · SUDBURY TOWN · ALPERTON

STANMORE · CANONS PARK · QUEENSBURY · KINGSBURY · PRESTON ROAD · SOUTH KENTON · NORTH WEMBLEY · WEMBLEY PARK · WEMBLEY for SUDBURY · NEASDEN · STONEBRIDGE PARK · DOLLIS HILL · WILLESDEN GREEN · HARLESDEN · KILBURN · WILLESDEN JUNCTION · WEST HAMPSTEAD · KENSAL GREEN · FINCHLEY ROAD · QUEENS PARK · KILBURN PARK · SWISS COTTAGE · MAIDA VALE · ST. JOHNS WOOD · WARWICK AVENUE · EDGWARE ROAD · BAKER STREET · MARYLEBONE

BUSHEY HEATH · ELSTREE · BROCKLEY HILL · EDGWARE · BURNT OAK WATLING · COLINDALE · HENDON CENTRAL · BRENT · GOLDERS GREEN · HAMPSTEAD · BELSIZE PARK · CHALK FARM · KENTISH TOWN · CAMDEN TOWN · MORNINGTON CRESCENT · EUSTON · GREAT PORTLAND STREET · WARREN STREET

MILL HILL EAST · MILL HILL THE HALE · EAST FINCHLEY · CRANLEY GARDENS · MUSWELL HILL · HIGHGATE · ARCHWAY · CROUCH END · TUFNELL PARK · STROUD GREEN · ARSENAL HIGHBURY HILL · HOLLOWAY ROAD · CALEDONIAN ROAD · KINGS CROSS ST. PANCRAS · ANGEL · OLD STREET

HIGH BARNET · TOTTERIDGE · WOODSIDE PARK · WEST FINCHLEY · FINCHLEY CENTRAL · ALEXANDRA PALACE · FINSBURY PARK · DRAYTON PARK · HIGHBURY & ISLINGTON · CANONBURY & ESSEX ROAD

COCKFOSTERS · OAKWOOD · SOUTHGATE · ARNOS GROVE · BOUNDS GREEN · WOOD GREEN · TURNPIKE LANE · MANOR HOUSE · MOORGATE · ALDERSGATE · FARRINGDON

ONGAR · BLAKE HALL · NORTH WEALD · EPPING · THEYDON BOIS · CHIGWELL LANE · LOUGHTON · BUCKHURST HILL · RODING VALLEY · CHIGWELL · GRANGE HILL · HAINAULT · FAIRLOP · BARKINGSIDE · NEWBURY PARK · WOODFORD · SOUTH WOODFORD GEORGE LANE · SNARESBROOK · REDBRIDGE · WANSTEAD · GANTS HILL · LEYTONSTONE · LEYTON · STRATFORD

PADDINGTON · LATIMER ROAD · WESTBOURNE PARK · LADBROKE GROVE · ROYAL OAK · UXBRIDGE ROAD · BAYSWATER · QUEENSWAY · MARBLE ARCH · REGENTS PARK · GOODGE STREET · RUSSELL SQUARE · EUSTON SQUARE · CHANCERY LANE GRAYS INN · HOLBORN KINGSWAY · ST. PAULS · BANK · LIVERPOOL STREET · SHOREDITCH · BETHNAL GREEN · MILE END · BOW ROAD

EALING BROADWAY · NORTH ACTON · WOOD LANE · WEST ACTON · EAST ACTON · SHEPHERDS BUSH · HOLLAND PARK · NOTTING HILL GATE · LANCASTER GATE · BOND STREET · OXFORD CIRCUS · TOTTENHAM COURT ROAD

EALING COMMON · SOUTH ACTON · GOLDHAWK ROAD · ADDISON ROAD · HIGH STREET KENSINGTON · GREEN PARK · PICCADILLY CIRCUS · COVENT GARDEN · LEICESTER SQUARE · CANNON STREET · TOWER HILL MONUMENT · ALDGATE EAST · ALDGATE · STEPNEY GREEN · WHITECHAPEL · SHADWELL · WAPPING · ROTHERHITHE · SURREY DOCKS

HOUNSLOW WEST · HOUNSLOW EAST · BOSTON MANOR · SOUTH EALING · ACTON TOWN · HAMMERSMITH · BARONS COURT · KNIGHTSBRIDGE · HYDE PARK CORNER · GLOUCESTER ROAD · SLOANE SQUARE · TRAFALGAR SQUARE · STRAND · ALDWYCH · TEMPLE · MANSION HOUSE · BLACKFRIARS · LONDON BRIDGE · BOROUGH

HOUNSLOW CENTRAL · OSTERLEY · NORTHFIELDS · CHISWICK PARK · TURNHAM GREEN · STAMFORD BROOK · RAVENSCOURT PARK · WEST KENSINGTON · EARLS COURT · SOUTH KENSINGTON · VICTORIA · ST. JAMES PARK · CHARING CROSS · WESTMINSTER

GUNNERSBURY · WEST BROMPTON · WALHAM GREEN · PARSONS GREEN · PUTNEY BRIDGE · EAST PUTNEY · SOUTHFIELDS · WIMBLEDON PARK · WIMBLEDON · KEW GARDENS · RICHMOND

WATERLOO · LAMBETH NORTH · KENNINGTON · ELEPHANT & CASTLE · OVAL · STOCKWELL · CLAPHAM NORTH · CLAPHAM COMMON · CLAPHAM SOUTH · BALHAM · TRINITY ROAD TOOTING BEC · TOOTING BROADWAY · COLLIERS WOOD · SOUTH WIMBLEDON MERTON · MORDEN

NEW CROSS GATE · NEW CROSS

TO BROMLEY · WEST HAM · PLAISTOW · UPTON PARK · EAST HAM · BARKING · UPNEY · BECONTREE · HEATHWAY · DAGENHAM · ELM PARK · HORNCHURCH · UPMINSTER BRIDGE · UPMINSTER

RIVER THAMES

LINES TO BE ELECTRIFIED ▬ ▬ ▬
LINES UNDER CONSTRUCTION ● ● ● ●

LONDON TRANSPORT

H. C. BECK

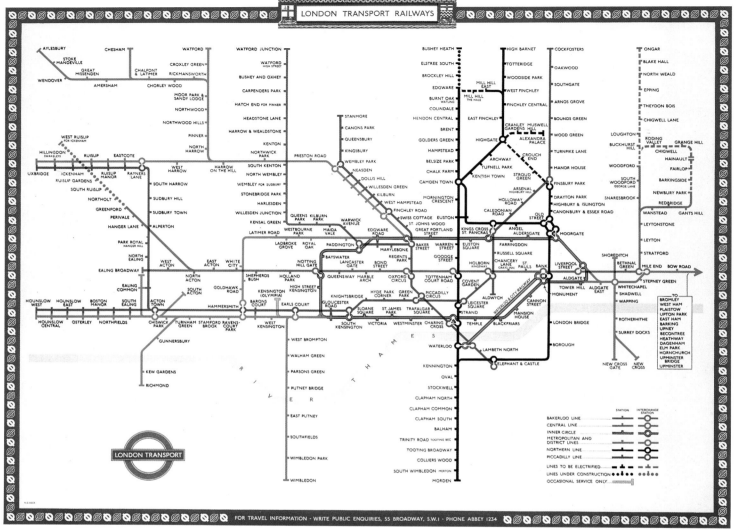

LONDON TRANSPORT

31 Quad royal poster of 1949 (right). Beck considered this perhaps the best of all his versions of the Diagram. The Metropolitan and District Lines were now shown in different colours, the Metropolitan reverting to purple while the District remained green. The Inner Circle had been renamed the Circle Line and given its own colour – yellow – while retaining the black outline on its inner edge which had been introduced in 1947. This was not, of course, a truly separate line, being serviced jointly by the Metropolitan and District. The Central Line was now completed to West Ruislip in the west and as far as Loughton in the east. There was a reorientation of lines around Baker Street and Paddington, where the Bakerloo Line slipped inside those two stations (though this did not survive the next edition). A proposed extension of the Bakerloo Line from Elephant & Castle to Camberwell was included for the first time and rings with white-line connectors were added at Rayners Lane (Metropolitan/Piccadilly), at Ealing Common (District/Piccadilly) and at South Kensington (District/Piccadilly). The eastward route of the Metropolitan and District Lines was now drawn as far as Barking, where previously it had only been drawn to Bow Road.

30 Quad foolscap (27 x 34in/686 x 863mm) poster of 1947. A significant, if unsensational, innovation appeared in this edition: the outlining of those parts of the District and Metropolitan Lines which constituted the Inner Circle – not a separately acknowledged line at this time but now identified on the Diagram for the first time. The thickened route lines with their names shown in white within them, seen on the 1946 quad royal poster, were not used here; nor was the 'rectification' of the stretch of the Metropolitan and Bakerloo Lines between Baker Street and Wembley Park, which remained a diagonal here.

40

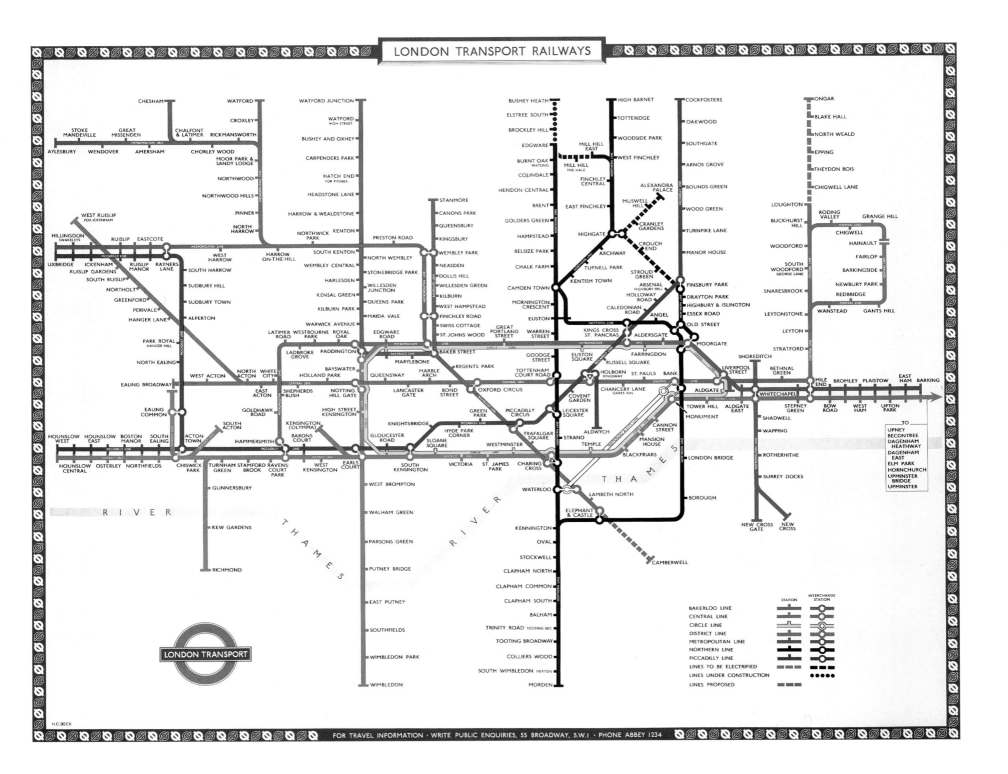

LONDON TRANSPORT RAILWAYS

LONDON TRANSPORT

	STATION	INTERCHANGE STATION
BAKERLOO LINE		
CENTRAL LINE		
CIRCLE LINE		
DISTRICT LINE		
METROPOLITAN LINE		
NORTHERN LINE		
PICCADILLY LINE		
LINES TO BE ELECTRIFIED		
LINES UNDER CONSTRUCTION		
LINES PROPOSED		

TO—
UPNEY
BECONTREE
DAGENHAM
HEATHWAY
DAGENHAM
EAST
ELM PARK
HORNCHURCH
UPMINSTER
BRIDGE
UPMINSTER

H.C. BECK

32 A quad royal poster of 1952 (opposite), virtually identical to the 1951 maps, in which the proposed northward extensions of the Northern Line had been omitted, as was the proposed extension of the Bakerloo Line from Elephant & Castle to Camberwell. Rings with white-line connectors were added at Gloucester Road (Piccadilly/District). The Richmond branch of the District Line reverted to a diagonal and a matching diagonal kink was built into the Thames so that the town now lay alongside the river. The most significant change was the introduction of a reference grid. Comprising 4 x 6 squares it was not overly intrusive.

the District and Metropolitan Lines (both of which, incidentally, had been shown as green since 1937*) — that delineated it clearly for the first time, by means of a black outline round the green.

In 1947 Beck was tempted by the offer of a teaching post at the London School of Printing and Kindred Trades, soon to be amalgamated with the LCC School of Photo-engraving and Lithography and renamed the London School of Printing and the Graphic Arts. His job at London Transport held no great prospect of advancement, congenial though it was, and he resigned in order to join the staff of the School. The subjects he was called on to teach were the theory and practice of typographic design, colour theory, the history of type design, lettering and general drawing.

This was a period of new thinking in graphic design in Britain (the very term itself only came into general use at this time). The painter William Johnstone, having made a great success as principal of Camberwell School of Art & Craft, had just been appointed to the same role at the Central School of Arts & Crafts, which had not had a full time principal since the outbreak of World War 2. He brought with him graphic designer Jesse Collins as head of the Department of Book Design and Production, who in his turn recruited as teachers Anthony Froshaug† and Herbert Spencer. Both of them were great enthusiasts for a subject which became known much later as 'information design'; and their often quoted paradigm in this area was the Underground Diagram. Meanwhile, in this same year, Robin Darwin was appointed principal of the Royal College of Art and Design and set about revitalising it with special reference to its original purpose of training designers for industry; one of his key appointments was that of Richard Guyatt as head of the School of Graphic Arts. As a practising graphic designer, Guyatt, too, was concerned to promote a more purposeful, less dilettante approach to graphic design.

Beck became aware, perhaps for the first time, of the ramifications of this subject. As the likes of Collins, Froshaug, Spencer and Guyatt were making the connection between the pictorial aspects of the graphic arts and the more down-to-earth concerns represented by the Diagram, so was he. Meanwhile, he was as absorbed as ever with the more or less continuous task of updating and improving it. The Becks' whole house would be strewn with the clutter of work in progress, even the bedroom: Nora, his wife, would find little

piles of sketches under his pillow when she made the bed in the morning. And his niece, Joan Baker, recalls seeing very large copies of the Diagram covering the living room carpet as he crawled over them making amendments.

It is difficult to avoid the analogy of this ongoing involvement with the Diagram being equivalent to that of a father for his favourite child — escaping from his firm control from time to time by someone else's unlooked-for influence but always returning to the guidance of his firm hand.

By the 1949 edition (31) some crucial modifications had been made: the Inner Circle, now known as the Circle Line, was shown as a separate route line in yellow, strengthened with a black outline on its inner edge; the Metropolitan Line had its distinctive purple restored to it once more; the route lines were thickened to include (on the posters, that is) the names of the routes in white within them with the effect of making the whole Diagram bolder and more colourful.

Beck told the writer he considered this to be perhaps the best of all his versions of the Diagram, and it is not difficult to see why he thought so. With this design he had managed at last to eradicate all those features with which he had been unwillingly saddled by others — with the single exception of the thickened route lines, though he had become reconciled to them by now. He had incorporated a most welcome touch of yellow for the Circle Line; and he had achieved at last the degree of rectilinearity he believed appropriate to the Diagram as he had always conceived it. The one important omission was that he had not found a suitable way to incorporate the stretch of the District Line eastward from Barking to its terminus at Upminster.

Editions from 1951, such as the one illustrated (32), were of simpler design, by virtue of the omission of the proposed Northern Line extensions from Finsbury Park, Mill Hill East and Edgware, and the Bakerloo Line extension from Elephant & Castle to Camberwell. Though this removed a few diagonal lines from the Diagram, which would have pleased Beck given his desire for rectilinearity, at the same time we find him reintroducing a diagonal where he had only recently contrived a vertical. The District Line branch from Turnham Green to Richmond had become a vertical

* First seen on card folder No 2 of that year.

† Froshaug recommended Beck to the writer when the latter was his student in 1953, and this led to their first meeting.

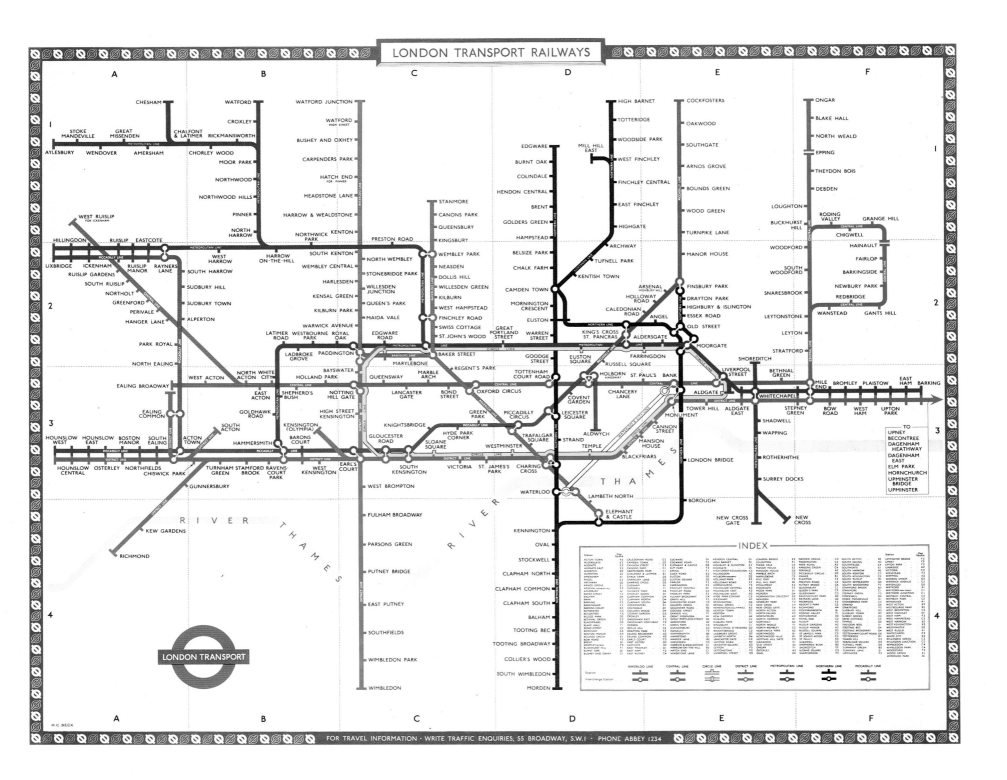

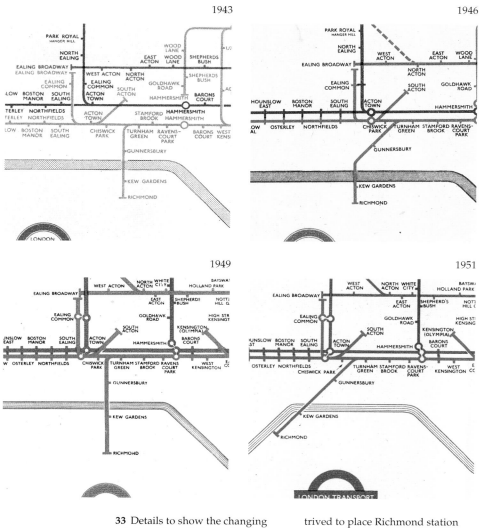

in 1943, had acquired a diagonal/vertical kink in 1946, and had once more become vertical in 1949; now it was once again a diagonal (**33**). This could have been under pressure from his bosses, who may have pointed out that Richmond was on the Thames, whereas his 1949 version implied it was some way to the south of the river. At any rate, he brought back a bend in the Thames, creating a diagonal which then matched the reinstated diagonal of the branch line. Richmond was once more restored to its rightful place.

However, such diagonal diversions were not to be put up with for very long. By 1954, Beck had 'rectified' the river itself: the Richmond branch could now revert to a vertical and lie alongside the river (**34**). More significantly, he had eliminated the diagonals on the eastern side of the Inner Circle, turning it into a clean rectangle with rounded corners. And most importantly of all, he had found a way, by means of the two right-angle bends in the route line, of incorporating the whole eastward extent of the District Line as far as Upminster, though he was not entirely happy with this solution since it conveyed the idea that Upminster is close to the Thames, whereas it is some six miles to the north.

There was another change in the 1954 design which is easy to overlook but which Beck considered substantial. He had always felt that, where a line branches, there should be a way of showing the branching that does not imply one arm is more important than the other. Now, in the case of the branches on the Northern Line north of Camden Town, on the Metropolitan Line west of Harrow-on-the-Hill, and a number of smaller instances, he had been able to achieve this; and incidentally, where the Metropolitan Line branches south of Surrey Docks, to New Cross Gate and New Cross, he managed to remove another diagonal into the bargain.

Gratuitous grid?

The introduction of a locating grid, tentatively at first, with a 24 square version in the 1951 and 1952 (**32**) poster editions, then with a much more noticeable 176 square version in the 1955 editions of both poster and card folder, was a mixed blessing. For those who did not want to use it for locating a station it was mere noise; and of course it required a large, space-devouring key panel on the poster. Beck was always in two minds about it. He couldn't deny its usefulness, and in fact he had seriously considered advocating its use when

33 Details to show the changing relationship of Richmond station and the River Thames over an eight year period. It was not until the 1951 version that Beck contrived to place Richmond station adjacent to the river, where it properly should have been, and indeed where it had been until 1943.

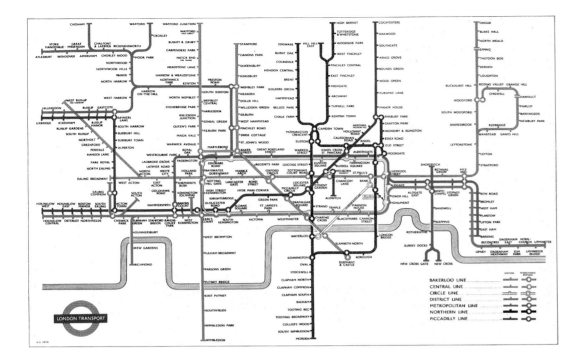

34 Card folder of 1954. With this edition Beck revised the design extensively to accommodate four new features: the 'rectification' of the River Thames; the simplification of the Circle Line from an irregular polygon to a clean rectangle; a treatment of the branching points of many lines to give each of those branches equal importance; and the appreciable thickening of the route lines. The rectilinear transformation of the river line, which had until then been a combination of horizontals and diagonals, was questionable. It did not assist Beck's quest for increasing rectilinearity in the route lines themselves except in the single case of the Richmond branch of the District Line which could now be a vertical and could also lie alongside the river (see **33**), and to some eyes it looked too utterly mechanical for such a natural feature. The simplified configuration of the Circle Line was a decided improvement, though Beck said later that he preferred Garbutt's 'vacuum flask' shape for this feature (see **42**). The branching treatment had a significant effect on the general appearance of the Diagram, not least in that it disrupted the straight line between Edgware and Morden on the Northern Line: a carefully contrived vertical axis Beck had introduced in 1943 to match the horizontal axis of the Central Line which had been a key feature of the Diagram from the beginning. The reason for the thickening of the route lines is not immediately apparent from the card folder version, for the simple reason that it related to the re-introduction of the names of the lines in white lettering within them on the quad royal poster of the same year (see **35**). It could be argued that there was no need for the route lines on the card folder to be thickened just to match those on the poster, and that it would have been preferable to retain the greater elegance of the previous edition.

it was suggested to him by his father in 1933, but had resisted it for 20 years because he feared it would interrupt the clean flow of the route lines. Having concurred in the introduction of a 4 x 6 co-ordinate grid in 1951, he could not reasonably claim, on that evidence, that it was intrusive; but in 1955 he found he was implementing a more complex, 11 x 16, grid. Such a profusion of reference squares was both unnecessary and intrusive, especially in the card folders (and it is worth remarking that, between 1984 and 1988, the grid was progressively simplified to a 6 x 9 co-ordinate without any appreciable loss of usefulness and with a considerable improvement in appearance).

Beck was stuck with the over-elaborate reference grid throughout his remaining years of designing the Diagram. Though its inclusion was made with his full agreement, he confessed to the writer later that he wished he had resisted it, especially in relation to the more cluttered format of the card folder where, in any case, the user had to turn from front to back in order to relate the grid to the alphabetic list of stations. To compound the difficulty, the type size of the list was so small that it was very hard to read, especially in less than ideal lighting conditions.

Consolidation

From 1955 to 1959 (**35**, **36**, **37**), the year of Beck's last design* (**38**), the Diagram changed very little. However, he had completely redrawn it: all the curves in the route lines were tighter, though this is apparent only to the most sharp-eyed observer. No convincing reason can be adduced for this alteration and the writer is completely at a loss to understand its motivation, particularly in view of the many hours of handwork it must have entailed. Other minor changes were: the deletion of the South Acton branch on the District Line; the re-lettering of the escalator connection operating between Monument and Bank stations, probably because in the 1955 version it was too small to be readable; and the identification by lettering of the River Thames — the first time Beck had thought this necessary in the card folder version of the Diagram, though it had been included as a matter of course in the quad royal posters.

---

* Strictly speaking, the date on the last published version – a card folder – was March 1960.

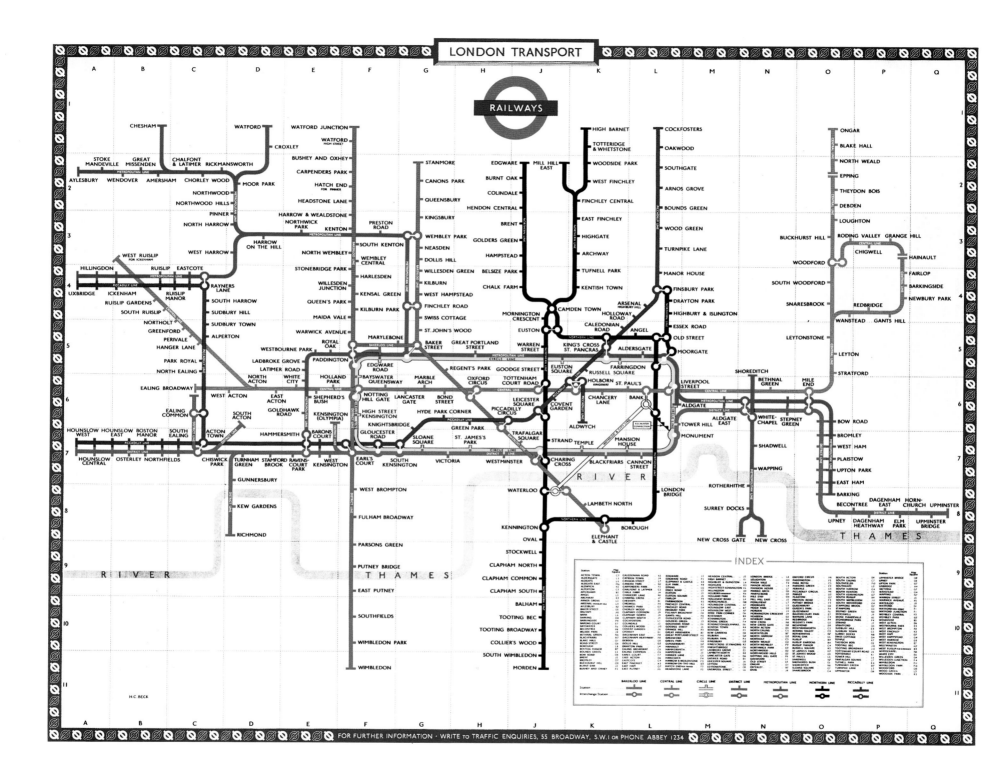

35 Quad royal poster of 1956 (left), showing how the route lines were thickened to incorporate their names within them in white lettering, a throwback to the designs of 1935-37. In addition to the new features already noted in the 1954 card folder (see **34**), the poster included a revamped reference grid of 11 x 16 squares, as against the much less intrusive 4 x 6 grid introduced in 1951. This was a doubtful modification, and one that Beck regretted in retrospect, though at the time it seemed appropriate to his continuing search for an ever more informative design.

36, 37 Card folders of 1957 (above right) and 1959 (below right). Though identical at first glance, a closer inspection reveals that the 1959 edition was completely redrawn. For no obvious reason Beck decided to tighten all the curves on the route lines. This change is most apparent in the branching above Camden Town on the Northern Line. It is difficult to see why the redrawing of all the curves – a most exacting and time-consuming exercise – was seen as an improvement worthy of the effort. Intriguingly, the curves of the River Thames were made more generous in the 1959 edition.

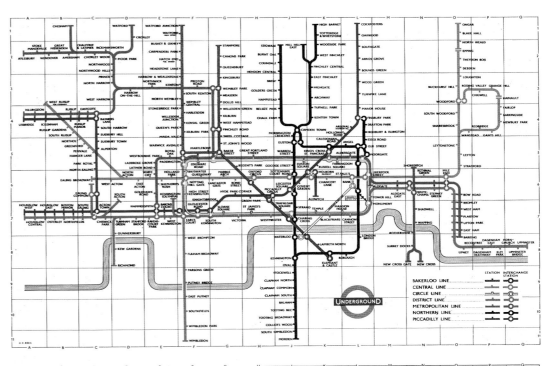

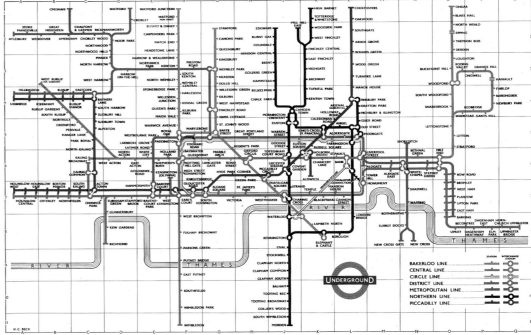

47

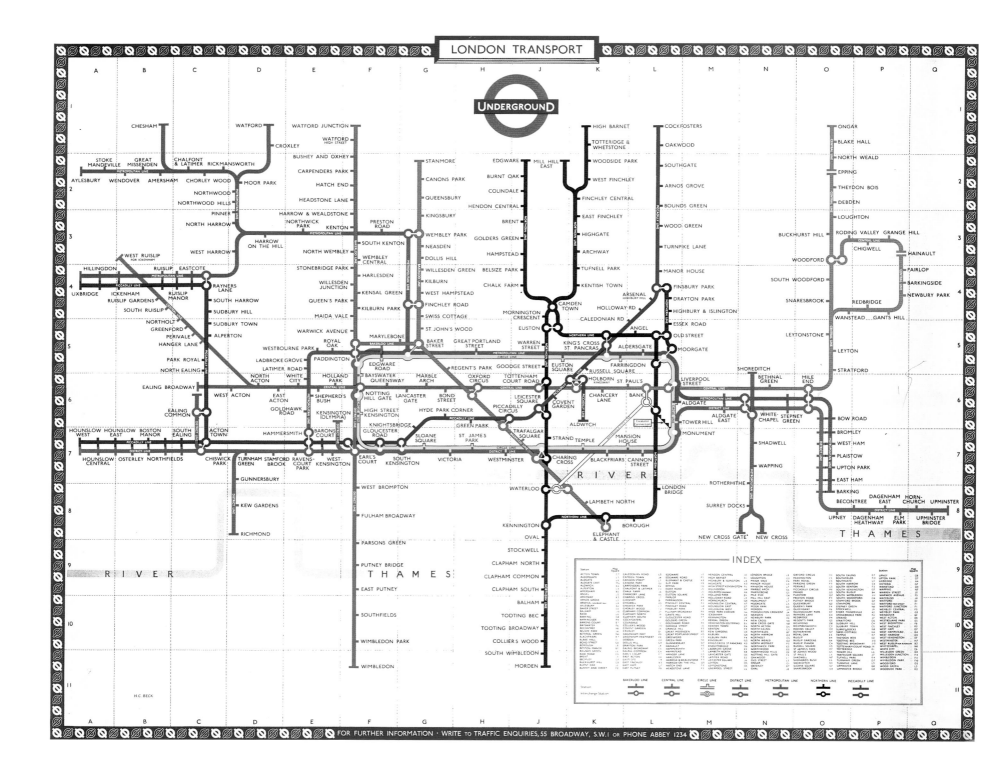

Fine tuning or just fiddling about?

Among the minor changes and adjustments noted above, only one — the deletion of the South Acton branch — was the result of a physical change in the network itself; the others could be classified as a species of fine tuning. Beck's long custodianship of the Diagram had understandably induced in him a passion for detail that sometimes appeared obsessive. One of the less significant features of the Underground network was the escalator linking Monument and Bank stations (**39**). First announced in September 1933, the prominent notice given to this took the form of a large box with the words 'Escalator connection between Bank and Monument Stations' in Johnston capitals appreciably larger than the station names themselves, from which extended a pointer to a broken-line link between the station rings. This continued until 1937, when the box was made smaller; the lettering also was smaller, simplified to 'Escalator connection' and no longer reversed out of a dark ground. By 1940 the box had disappeared and the broken line had become a zigzag line with the single word 'Escalator' alongside it; in 1943 the zigzag line had shrunk almost to nothing and the lettering had disappeared. By 1946, Monument station had

been repositioned so close to Bank station that there was no room for even a minimal indication; and it was not until 1954, with the redrawing of the Circle Line as a rectangle, that it could once more be shown. This time it was as three solid triangles representing a flight of stairs, accompanied by the minute lettering already referred to.

Though some of the changes to this feature were required by the adjustments to the general geometry of the Diagram, others were more in the nature of experiments or even — dare it be said? — whims. And if so, why not? None of these flights of fancy ever interfered with the clarity of the essential information; and for the *aficionados* of the Diagram they are an incidental delight.

But the minor adjustments and fine tuning which had preoccupied Beck for the last four years were small potatoes compared to the task he was already looking forward to with keen anticipation. In the late 1950s, planning was at an advanced stage for the Victoria Line, the first completely new Tube line since the opening of the 'Hampstead Tube' in 1907. Beck was anxious to begin the preliminary work involved in adjusting the Diagram to accommodate the new line. The challenge, he believed, would provide a new lease of life for the Diagram, and for its designer.

38 Quad royal poster of 1959. Though of course he was not aware of it at the time, this was to be Beck's last published poster version of the Diagram. Based on the same artwork as the 1956 edition and in most respects identical, it offers a 'spot-the-difference' opportunity for the eagle-eyed and a demonstration of Beck's ongoing passion for fine tuning. Apart from the obvious deletion resulting from the closing of the under-used shuttle between Acton Town and South Acton on the District Line, the following small changes have been detected: an extra white-line connector added at Charing Cross, between the Northern and Bakerloo Lines; the words 'Escalator Connection' between Monument and Bank stations changed from caps to upper-and-lower case; abbreviation of 'Caledonian Road' and 'Holloway Road' to 'Caledonian Rd' and 'Holloway Rd', a unique concession not previously allowed to Beck; 'Camden Town' altered from single line to double line setting; ampersand in 'Totteridge & Whetstone' moved from beginning of second line to end of first line (why?); 'Leicester Square' rearranged so that 'Square' was centred under 'Leicester' rather than ranged left; 'St James's Park' changed to 'St Jame's Park', an inexplicable mistake for which heads would have been hung in shame when it was revealed – too late; and lastly, 'Railways' in the roundel changed to 'Underground', easily missed though it was the largest lettering on the poster.

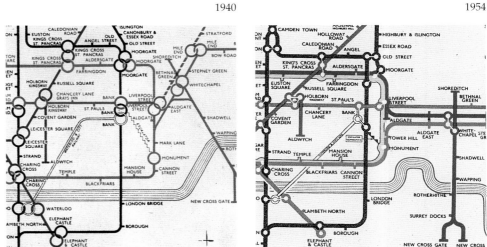

1937   1940   1954

39 Changing styles in representing the escalator link between Monument and Bank stations. For its first appearance, see **18**.

Chapter 5

Rejection

40 Quad royal poster (opposite) dated November 1962 and with 'Designed by Harold F Hutchison'. This is the same as the design which first appeared in April 1960, except that the earlier edition did not include the Victoria Line. Hutchison's usurping version contained the following similarities to the Beck originals: use of horizontals, verticals and diagonals; expansion of the central area in relation to outlying portions of the diagram; use of 'ticks' to denote stations along route lines; colour coding differentiating the lines; elimination of all surface features except for the River; use of the Central Line as the horizontal axis of the design. The main differences were: elimination of all curves on route lines; substitution of upper-and-lower case lettering in place of capitals, except for interchange stations, and terminal stations; use of rings and squares to differentiate those having British Railways connections (the squares) from those which do not; inclusion of symbols to signify stations with restricted use; drastic simplification of the use of interchange symbols in linked multiples, so that nowhere were there more than two together. The general configuration had far more diagonals than Beck Diagrams of the last 22 years; on the other hand it shared many characteristics in common with Beck Diagrams of the period 1933-38.

At the beginning of 1960, Beck appears to have had no reason to believe he would not continue his freelance relationship with London Transport in regard to any new versions of the Diagram that might be necessary. Although, as we have seen, he had not received an absolute assurance in writing on this point from either Barman himself or succeeding Publicity Officers, neither had he any suggestion from them that he would not continue to be involved.

However, certain doubts were being expressed in the late 1950s about the severely rectilinear form of Beck's current designs. By some, Publicity Officer Harold F Hutchison in particular it seems, Beck was felt to be a difficult man, not easy to deal with*. Moves were once again made to take the Diagram away from him.

Thus it was that Beck was confronted, in spring 1960 (**40**), by a version with which he had had no involvement whatever. The shock was in no way mitigated by the discovery that the design was signed by Hutchison himself, a person not known to him as a designer; but the most distressing feature of all was the amateurish inadequacy of the new Diagram. How could London Transport have lent itself to such a travesty of all the Beck design stood for? The lettering was cramped in many places, most bizarrely where 'Aldgate' was split into 'Ald' on one side of the route line and 'gate' on the other. Although Hutchison had permitted himself the use of upper-and-lower-case, when it had not been allowed to Beck, he still found himself compelled to abbreviate many station names (for example, 'Trafalgar Sq', 'Liverpool St' and 'Bow Rd'), another convenience not previously permitted by London Transport† (but see caption **38**). The most unforgivable feature was the elimination, or more precisely, avoidance, of all curves in the drawing of the route lines. The result was disturbingly jerky, quite different to the effortless flow that Beck always managed to achieve.

To add insult to injury a press release from Hutchison's own office dated 19.4.60 declared:

NEW MAP FOR THE LONDON UNDERGROUND – CHANGE OF STYLE AFTER 30 YEARS

London Transport's famous diagrammatic poster map of the Underground, familiar to Londoners and visitors for the last 30 years, has been given a complete 'new look'.

The new-style map is now going up at London's 279 Underground stations. It is easier to read — only main interchange stations are shown in capital letters, and these specially marked to indicate interchange with British Railways or other Underground lines; it is more geographical in the layout of the seven lines and travel information for passengers to air terminals, London Airport and main line stations is given for the first time...

It will be noticed that the press release stated unequivocally that the new version 'is easier to read'; yet so far as we know no tests were conducted to prove this contention and there could have been little basis for such a bald assertion.

Beck's first written reaction was to Christian Barman. His letter of 14 May 1960 reads, in full:

Dear Mr Barman,

You have of course seen the new printing of the 'Underground' diagram, and I hope you will so appreciate my feelings as to take

---

* In a conversation with the writer in February 1994, Paul E Garbutt, a senior member of the LT staff for many years, remembers Beck as 'a rather fretful person' when they met once in the Publicity Office.

† It is worth recording that there was a general move away from capital letters for signing at the time, as shown with the UK Motorway signs from 1959, London bus blinds from 1961 and British Rail station signs from 1962.

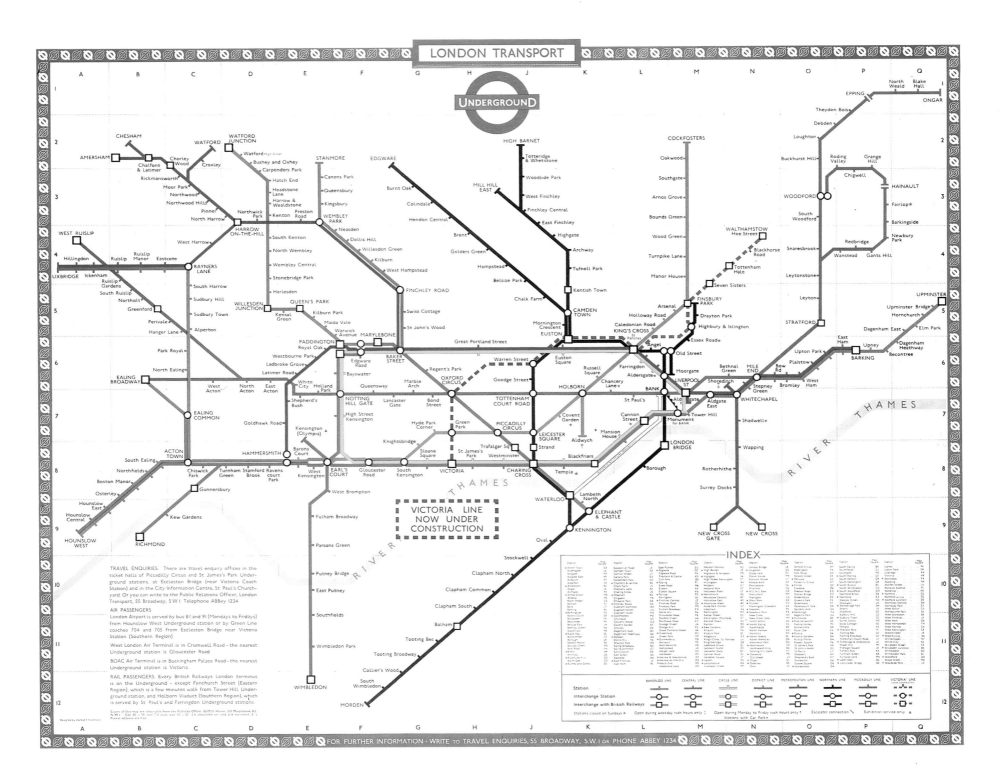

51

the vehemence of some of the following remarks with a pinch of salt!

I am afraid I see this as just an untidy modification of my 1939 edition — but whatever one may think of the merits of it, it certainly places me in a dilemma.

Unaware of this 'do-it-yourself' departure, I have been working for some time on a new diagram, but how can I now have confidence in the officer to whom I am supposed to submit the design?

You will remember that the idea of converting the old 'vermicelli' into a diagram was entirely mine, and that the fee agreed on the transfer of copyright was a nominal one on condition that all future work on the diagram was to be carried out or edited by me, and my name always to appear.

Because of the happy memories I have of those days back at '55' I am most reluctant to put you to any trouble on my behalf, but I should be most grateful for a word from you confirming to me that the undertaking given to me by you as the then Publicity Officer is still to be regarded as binding.

Barman's reply was prompt but only mildly sympathetic:

Dear Beck

It was nice to hear from you again, but I am sorry you did not have a pleasanter reason for writing.

Like you, I have seen the new Underground diagram, and I think it is a pretty poor job. But I am afraid my knowledge of your personal arrangements with the London Passenger Transport Board is a bit vague.

As you may remember, I was Publicity Officer from 1935 to 1941. Your diagram had been in existence for some time before I got there, and I do not think that any arrangement was actually made between yourself and myself. However, I remember your telling me that you had some arrangement of this kind, and when I myself had some ideas about a new version of the diagram I, of course, came to you. But I have no recollection of ever seeing anything in writing.

Why not have a quiet word with Bryce Beaumont, who was there in your time, and who may perhaps be able to make some suggestion? I am very sorry that my recollections do not look like being very helpful to you.

Beck took up Barman's suggestion and had a word with his old colleague and friend, Bryce Beaumont, by this time in a

responsible position in the Publicity Office. Beaumont, however, was most reluctant to express an opinion on the matter*. Beck wrote to Barman again, on 14 July 1960:

...After all this time I suppose I should not have expected you to recollect that meeting in November 1937 about the copyright. I remember well how horrified you were when you asked, and I told you, how much I was paid for the original design, and you did yourself make the suggestion that in return for the transfer of copyright I should receive a small fee, with a promise that in future all work on the diagram should be carried out or edited by me at proper commercial rates; also that the only written confirmation of these conditions was contained in a memorandum from me to you shortly afterwards.

Mr Hutchison would, I imagine, be disinclined to consider in the present circumstances anything that I might submit, and in any case I have my own feelings of disinclination! I am astonished at the discourteous way in which he has seen fit to assume authorship of this world-famous five-guinea† design.

In a brief reply dated 15 July 1960, Barman wrote:

Thank you for your letter about the Underground diagram. I really am very sorry to have been of so little help to you in this matter.

I am surprised to find that the arrangement which you say I personally made with you in 1937 was not recorded on paper as far as I was concerned. However, if your memorandum to me sets out clearly what was agreed between us I see no reason why you should not send this to Mr. Hutchison.

This was the last word from Barman on the matter.

After a delay of some six months there ensued an increasingly acrimonious exchange of letters between Beck and Hutchison. It began with a request from Beck to have returned to him some drawings he had provided 'some time

---

* Beaumont's position in this matter, as second-in-command to Hutchison, was very delicate. He owed an over-riding loyalty to his employers yet at the same time he felt his friend Harry was being badly treated. In a recent correspondence with the writer he states: 'The one problem that has to be answered is whether Harry's drawing was a map or a diagram. Where I think Hutchison was grievously at fault was to think the design could be both. I often feel that my part in the affair was pusillanimous and culpable in that I was never able to convince Hutchison that he was wrong both in his personal treatment of Beck and in the design of the diagram.'

† In fact, ten guineas was paid – see caption on page 19.

back...dealing with the proposed Victoria Line', but also contained the paragraph:

Would you kindly note the following facts for your records, if they are not there already. The Underground railways diagram which has been exhibited on London Transport properties since 1932 [sic] was originated by me in 1931. I was paid, I think, five guineas for the design first published, and the copyright remained with me. In 1937, in return for my signature on a copyright form, I was given an undertaking that all future designing work on the Underground diagram would be given to me to do or edit, and that my name would always appear on it.

In his reply, dated two days later, Hutchison wrote:

My dear Beck

Thank you for your letter of 14 January ... I am not aware of any undertaking by my predecessors, but I shall be very happy to use your work again whenever a job arrives which would suit you.

There followed a sequence of a dozen letters to Hutchison, and a dozen replies from him, in the same vein but with a rising crescendo of bitterness from Beck and exasperation from Hutchison, culminating in a letter from the latter, dated 12 October 1961. It bore the signs of legal advice:

Dear Mr Beck

I am in receipt of your letter of 5 October. I have not made any attack on your integrity, either expressly or impliedly, at any time. I have always been willing to discuss with you outstanding points, including those contained in the correspondence, and once again I invite you to come and see me.

It is for you to accept this invitation, otherwise this matter cannot proceed. I am not willing to continue this correspondence.

Beck, of course, could not let the matter rest there. He took things to the top, with a letter, dated 29 November, to A B B Valentine, Chairman of the London Transport Executive (the body that had taken over the responsibility for running the Underground in 1948). It was accompanied by two quad royal visuals, one with and one without the proposed Victoria Line. One paragraph of the letter ran:

You will see that the design is in the form of two rough layouts in quad-royal size: one without the proposed Victoria Line and one with a simple local alteration to bring it in. I think that the colour I have used, lilac, would be distinctive in most kinds of lighting.

Valentine passed the letter over to R M Robbins, Chief Public Relations Officer. His reply of 11 December 1961 contained a disappointing reaction to the visuals:

...the Executive cannot give you approval or authority to show the designs you sent in with your letter, if for no other reason than that until authority to go ahead with the construction is received, the precise alignment will remain subject to review...I am returning the two designs which you were good enough to send.

In a further exchange of letters Beck tried to advance a case for reconsidering this outright rejection, but with no success. It became sadly evident that London Transport was not in the least interested in returning the responsibility for designing future versions of the Diagram to him.

A glimpse of what might have been

One of the two visuals — that including the Victoria Line — has very recently come to light once more (**41**). Though it never went into print, of course, it still deserves careful examination as it represents Beck's design work at its most ingenious. From this it appears that the strategy behind the two visuals was (a) to familiarise the travelling public with a Diagram so composed that, when the Victoria Line came to be included, it would be done without drastic revision of the design and (b) to design it so that the Victoria Line would appear as a straight diagonal, thus drawing the strongest possible attention to its designated, and subsequently actual, route. The basic structure of the visuals followed the rectilinear form of Beck's last published version but there were some significant modifications: three of the few remaining diagonals in the 1959 edition — the Central Line branch from North Acton to West Ruislip, the Bakerloo Line from Baker Street to Elephant & Castle, the Piccadilly Line from Piccadilly Circus as far as Finsbury Park — were 'rectified' in the two matched visuals, presumably in order to throw a stronger emphasis on the diagonal of the new Victoria Line; the River Thames, on the other hand was now rendered in

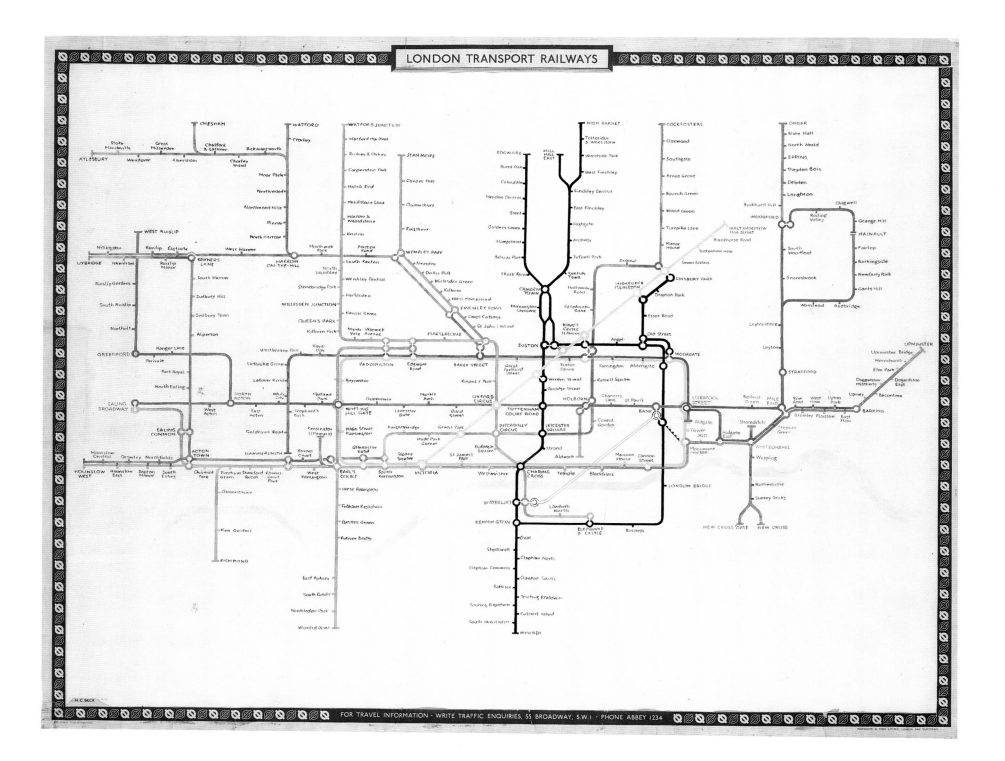

H.C.BECK

54

41 One of two quad royal visuals prepared by Beck during 1961 and submitted to London Transport Executive on 29 November of that year. Since both visuals were returned to him with a covering letter dated 11 December, and without comment, it may be assumed they were given no more than a cursory glance by the recipients. Had they taken a little more trouble and examined them carefully they would have discovered a most adroit proposition. Both visuals were identical except for the inclusion on one of them (shown here) of the proposed Victoria Line. Beck had completely revised the Diagram from his last published version so as to allow the new line – whenever the appropriate time arrived – to be displayed as a clean diagonal. This could have provided London Transport with a most effective device for promoting the use of the Victoria Line, which did indeed take a reasonable approximation to a diagonal course under London from Victoria to Walthamstow; meanwhile the matching version without the new line would accustom the public to the revised configuration onto which the Victoria Line was to be imposed. Instead, they settled for Hutchison's ham-fisted contrivance which took it on an awkward and unconvincing route around existing lines. Beck's choice of lilac for the Victoria Line is interesting to compare with the choice made independently by London Transport of violet, the latter being replaced by light blue at an early stage owing to difficulties in reproducing it on vitreous enamel signage.

rectilinear form; and the District Line from Whitechapel to Upminster was revised somewhat along the lines of Hutchison's version (the only aspect of that design of which Beck expressed approval*).

This unpublished design contained one other detail which, though minor, offers revealing evidence of Beck's passionate concern for detail: the Euston/Mornington Crescent/Camden Town stretch of the Northern Line. He had always had a sneaking feeling he hadn't done justice to a unique variable on this route. At this time the two branches coming down from Edgware and High Barnet took alternate routes after Camden Town: some trains went eastward through Euston to King's Cross and Bank, while other trains went south through Euston to Warren Street and Charing Cross; and of course, the same thing happened going north, except that the switch occurred at Euston. The real problem of diagrammatic representation was that all trains from High Barnet going south to Charing Cross stopped at Mornington Crescent, while all trains going eastward to Bank did not. Hitherto, Beck had compromised by merely showing Mornington Crescent on the left-hand loop, so as to imply that it lay along the line of the southward route to Charing Cross, even though the station itself would have appeared on the right in a true map. The dozens of drawings he did of this complex switch during the work on his 1961 visuals are a token of his obsession with accurate representation (see Appendix F). The configuration at which he arrived wasn't entirely to his satisfaction; he considered it only a marginal improvement on previous versions.

Although he received no official encouragement whatsoever to continue his design work on the Diagram, Beck persisted in making his case as strongly as ever, even after a letter from Robbins, dated 12 April 1962, put London Transport's opinion clearly enough:

Dear Mr Beck,

Thank you for your letter of 30 March. If at any time London Transport decides to use your map again, nobody but yourself will be commissioned to alter it and bring it up to date. The map now in use [that is, Hutchison's] *is of another design, and this is the one on which London Transport intends to show the Victoria Line and any other future additions to the Underground system.*

Beck's persistence, in spite of this unequivocal statement, resulted from his absolute conviction that the Hutchison diagram would be exposed, sooner rather than later, for the inadequate bodge-up it undoubtedly was; and that London Transport would have to come back to him, cap in hand, to ask him to put the Diagram back on the right tracks.

In his first assumption, he was entirely right; but in the second, he was sadly mistaken.

The first intimation that a third party was now involved came in a letter dated 5 November 1963 from Hutchison, in reply to yet another attempt by Beck to establish his right to future work on the Diagram:

Dear Beck

Underground Diagram

...Thank you for sending me your version of the Victoria Line. We have already commissioned and have already in production a completely new diagrammatic map, so I am returning your rough with this letter...

* Writing later of the Hutchison design, he said, 'I thought that the introduction of the sharp corners... did little to improve the design...[and] tended to give a 'stop-start' effect. I also considered the layout too crowded: names had to be abbreviated or divided. But I liked the treatment of the Upminster end.'

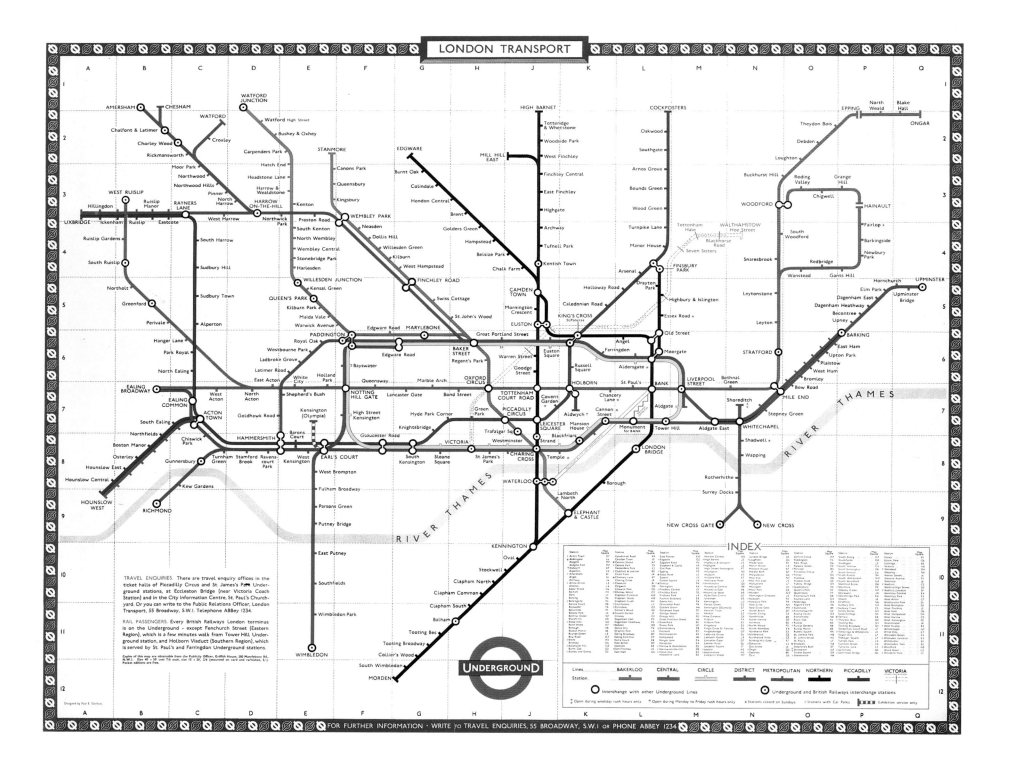

56

42 Quad royal poster dated March 1964 and signed 'Designed by Paul E Garbutt'. Begun as a sketch made at Christmas 1962 by a senior employee of London Transport who, like others of his colleagues, had a poor opinion of the Hutchison design, it was a very considerable improvement, restoring much needed curves to the route lines, eliminating the congestion at the eastern end of the Circle Line that pro-

duced the nonsense of having to place 'Ald' on one side of the route line and 'gate' on the other, and creating a distinctive shape for the Circle Line that was to become known, within London Transport, as the 'thermos flask'. Interchange symbols were printed black, as in the Hutchison version, rather than the colour of the Line, as in the Beck Diagram, but instead of the clumsy square employed by the

former to denote interchanges with British Rail stations, Garbutt introduced a new, neater device: a black dot within the standard interchange ring. But for all the differences embodied in this design it still shared with its immediate predecessor those close similarities to the Beck Diagram of 1933-38 which clearly demonstrated its inspiration.

being self-coloured, as in Beck's designs. This had the advantage of avoiding a difficult register of two colours, or three in the case of Paddington and Hammersmith, which had always been a printing problem for the Beck Diagrams, especially in the card folders, because of the small scale of reproduction. On the other hand, the greater prominence given to the interchange rings by printing them in black had the unwelcome effect of interrupting the flow of route lines.

In another respect Garbutt followed neither Beck nor Hutchison: he devised a new shape for the Circle Line. Where Beck had, by 1954, arrived at a rectangle with rounded corners, and Hutchison had reverted to an irregular polygon resembling Beck's earlier designs, Garbutt came up with a shape resembling a vacuum flask. More appropriate to the on-the-ground configuration than Beck's rectangle, yet more memorable than Hutchison's undistinguished polygon, it was a genuinely helpful feature which Garbutt retained in all his subsequent versions (including those incorporating the Victoria and Jubilee Lines) and which is still a distinctive part of the current Diagram.

While this version of the Diagram was in preparation, Beck wrote a very long letter to Robbins dated 7 April 1963, presenting his view of the history of the conception and development of the Diagram, restating yet again his claim to sole stewardship of the design. The last paragraphs of this letter are worth quoting in full since they show with painful clarity the apparent misapprehension under which he was labouring as to the nature of the new map Hutchison had spoken of in his letter of 5 November 1963:

Photograph: Godfrey Argent

Paul E Garbutt, photographed in 1969.

What had happened, unknown to Harry Beck until this moment, was as follows. In the winter of 1962 Paul E Garbutt, an employee of London Transport who had just been appointed Assistant Secretary and New Works Officer, decided to attempt, mainly in his spare time, a redesign of the Diagram (**42**). He was motivated by a realisation that the current version was by that time fairly universally disapproved of, and by his own strong dislike of it*. He restored the curves in the route lines and eliminated many of the kinks that had so disfigured the Hutchison version; he reinstated the white-line connector device for interchange stations such as Paddington, Euston, King's Cross and Waterloo; and re-established a clean, horizontal axis for the Central Line, with a similar vertical axis for the Northern Line, echoing, in this respect, Beck's versions of 1943-52. But he did not revert to the strongly rectilinear effect of the 1943-59 period, keeping a balance between horizontals, verticals and diagonals more reminiscent of Beck's Diagrams from 1933 to 1938.

In one respect Garbutt followed Hutchison: the rings denoting interchange stations were printed black, instead of

...I had been getting material together, over a long period, for a documented report to send to my solicitors, but, as I understand from Mr Hutchison that the map now in production is one bearing no resemblance whatever to my diagrams, I think that it may be taken to put a period to the reasons for my protests and bring an unhappy interlude to an end.

I now look forward to seeing the new map as a matter of interest, and I should be grateful for a word from you that if ever it is proposed to revive the 45- and 90-degree idea I may be favoured with the goodwill of those earlier years. May I suggest that I now be invited to visualize, in a preliminary way, a future diagram on

* During the 1994 conversation referred to earlier (see footnote on p 50) he recalled thinking of the Hutchison version as 'a total abomination'.

that basis, perhaps on the general lines of my earlier geographic-ally-disposed diagrams, so that a new design can be ready in good time for the opening of the Victoria Line.

In the circumstances I should be eternally grateful to you if, supposing it is practicable, any consideration of a return to the 45- and 90-degree basis could be deferred until such time as I shall no longer find myself in the ridiculous and unethical position of being in unequal competition with my client over the design of my own map. I have not been given any guidance on the point by Mr Hutchison, so I can only guess that the earlier 'geogram' is thought to be better than the simplified 'rectogram'. But I do feel that the straight Victoria Line is worth preserving, so I have tried to show, on the retouched black-and-white prints and detail, that the simplified layout is adaptable to a very considerable degree. Please understand, however, that I am just as ready to go right back to something approximating to my 1933 rendering.

If I may look forward to the pleasure of a talk with you some time, you may be sure that you will find me ready to offer the same enthusiastic co-operation as always in the past.

Was there something disingenuous about Beck's assumption that, if the new diagram were to be one 'bearing no resemblance whatever' to his own, it would not make use of the 45- and 90-degree basis? One suspects that perhaps there was, and that he hoped, even at this late stage, London Transport would think again about launching yet another rehash of his own Diagram using, of course, the 45-and 90-degree basis. The mention of sending a 'documented report to my solicitors' may also have been an attempt to forestall such a publication. If this was in fact the intention, it was both naive and too late. To clinch matters, Robbins reply, dated 29 April, left no doubt in the matter:

...I think the real question at issue is this: you say that any Underground diagram based on the 45 and 90 degree idea is really your map and that you have the right to design, and to be given credit for, any such map which is used by us. If I am right in thinking this is your position, then London Transport must say that it cannot accept your contention. Some years ago when we wanted the map thought about freshly, the Publicity Officer was asked to have a new design prepared. As he did it himself, it was duly accredited to him. When this map in turn required re-thinking because of the need to show the Victoria Line on it, another of the Board's Officers produced a fresh design, and this has been ap-proved and is now in production, and it will be credited to him. Both these designs subsequent to yours have been worked out afresh within the framework of certain traditional practices associated with London Transport design, adopting broadly the 45 and 90 degree convention (though in the forthcoming design a certain number of curves are used in place of angles).

Our position then, I think, is this: if you think you have been inadequately paid for work which has been commissioned from you by London Transport, then this is a matter which can be discussed and I hope satisfactorily resolved. But it is impossible to accept that there is a responsibility to you in respect of work which we have commissioned or obtained from other people.

Several statements in this letter were open to question but there was one which, as he confirmed later to the writer, Beck found absolutely without foundation. This was that designs subsequent to his had been worked out afresh 'within the framework of traditional practices associated with London Transport design, adopting broadly the 45 and 90 degree convention'. Insofar as this could be described as traditional, it was a 'tradition' established by Beck himself, and none other! One is left wondering what kind of legal advice Robbins could have been calling on when he gave himself to such a contention; for there can be no doubt that, by this stage, both parties were wording their letters with caution and under legal advice. But whereas London Transport could call on their tame barrister, Beck could do no such thing. All the more puzzling, then, that LT should be putting forward, through Robbins, such an obviously questionable argument. On the basis of Robbins' letter their case looked decidedly dodgy, and one suspects they themselves were not unaware of this; but they had money and staying power, and they knew Beck had neither. Anyway, the fat was in the fire: even as Beck read Robbins' letter, copies of the new design were being distributed for posting at the 270-odd Underground stations.

When Harry Beck saw the first edition of the Garbutt Diagram on its appearance in May 1964, he had mixed feelings. One part of him was relieved to know that the depressing awfulness of the Hutchison version was to be replaced and that he would no longer have to suffer the embarrassment of an object that was such a ghastly parody of his own design; the other part of him despaired, because the replacement was obviously more accomplished and had restored some of the design qualities of his own work. Yet it was not his, and was signed by someone else who made no acknowledgement of the — to him — staring fact that it was very largely derived from Beck's own work. During the currency of the Hutchison version there was always the hope that, when they saw the error of their ways, London Transport would ask him to resume his work on the Diagram; now they had a much better design by another hand, and Beck's chances of being consulted once more were extremely remote.

Garbutt's design added more fuel to Beck's anger and bitterness over what he believed to be a betrayal, since it resembled his original even more than Hutchison's had done; and this, in spite of the assurances he had been given, prior to its appearance, that this would be 'a completely new diagrammatic map' (Hutchison, in his letter of 5 November 1963 already quoted). On the basis of legal advice that he had a *prima facie* case against London Transport, Beck now faced the prospect of a strenuous law suit, should he wish to pursue what he believed to be his rightful claim for redress. However, by this time both he and his wife, Nora, were feeling the effects of three and a half years of anxiety and frustration. Nora, especially was very depressed and pessimistic about the outcome of what could be an expensive and fruitless legal confrontation.

Beck's last shot

While he hesitated to come to a decision about further legal involvement, Harry embarked once more on a version of the Diagram (**43**), this time taking into account the existence of the Garbutt design. This was to be his last bid for acceptance by London Transport. He adopted the more geographically relevant configuration used by Garbutt (which was, after all, very close to his own early designs of the 1930s) and also the adapted symbols Garbutt had used for the interchange stations. His intention was to show that the Garbutt/Beck configuration (as he saw it) could be adapted to incorporate the simple diagonal line he had already employed for the proposed Victoria Line. That concept was entirely his and must surely be accepted as such by London Transport.

In conversation with the writer in later years, Nora Beck recalled her husband's obsessive work on the Diagram during this period as though it were a sort of therapy. There were the same piles of pencil sketches on the bedside table,

even under the bed, and the same full size quad royal visuals all over the living room floor, as there had been since 1933. Now, however, there was a sense of unreality about Beck's continuing devotion to the task, since he could have had little, if any, expectation of his work achieving publication. The design that emerged, however, was very far from being merely a therapeutic indulgence: confident, ingenious and deceptively simple, it had all of his customary authority. He had taken the current Garbutt design and transformed it into his own — or as he might have said, back into his own. He felt compelled to accept the Hutchison/Garbutt convention of the black printing of the interchange rings, even though he continued to have reservations about the resulting interruption of the route line flow. But he kept the concept of a clean diagonal for the proposed Victoria Line, though, unaccountably, he gave it a little turn to the horizontal between Finsbury Park and the terminal at Walthamstow. While retaining Garbutt's general shape for the Circle Line, he added a hump to its upper right shoulder, bringing King's Cross St Pancras level with Euston, facilitating the placing of those stations along the diagonal of the Victoria Line.

The King's Cross complex occupied a great deal of Beck's thinking on this version of the Diagram, as indeed it had on the two versions he had sent to Valentine, Chairman of the London Transport Executive, on 29 November 1961, before the revelation of the Garbutt design. In the earlier versions he had used the self-coloured rings with the white-line connectors that he had employed with such success since 1946; now he had to adhere to the black-printed variation favoured by Garbutt. If we compare a sketch of his 1961 solution to the King's Cross complex with a sketch of his 1964 equivalent, it is seen that, in the earlier version he represented the five lines intersecting here — the Northern, Piccadilly, Metropolitan, Circle and proposed Victoria — with four self-coloured rings (the Metropolitan and Circle sharing one ring, half of it purple and half yellow). In the later version he used only three (black) rings, one for the Piccadilly, one for the Metropolitan/Circle, and one for the proposed Victoria, but none for the Northern. In this he was probably attempting the sort of simplification exercised by Garbutt, who was using only two rings for four lines (the proposed Victoria Line was not yet being indicated on published versions). But the Beck variants of 1961 and 1964 were

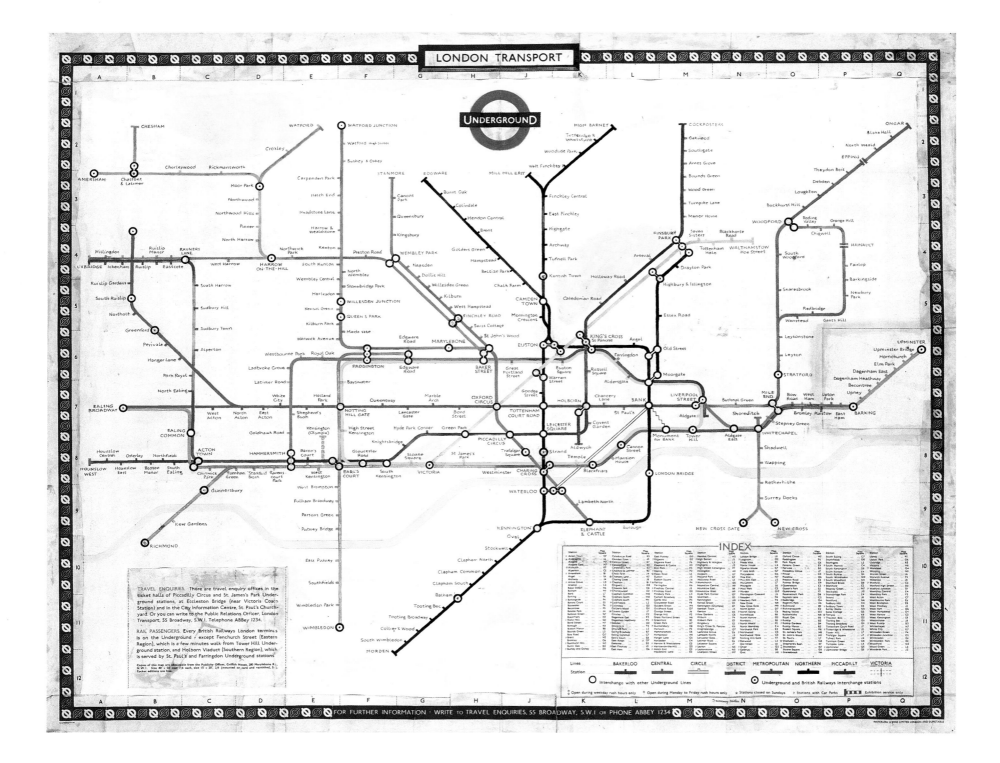

UNDERGROUND

TRAVEL ENQUIRIES. There are travel enquiry offices in the ticket halls of Piccadilly Circus and St. James's Park Underground stations, at Eccleston Bridge (near Victoria Coach Station) and in the City Information Centre, St. Paul's Churchyard. Or you can write to the Public Relations Officer, London Transport, 55 Broadway, S.W.I. Telephone ABBey 1234.

RAIL PASSENGERS. Every British Railways London terminus is on the Underground - except Fenchurch Street (Eastern Region), which is a few minutes walk from Tower Hill Underground station, and Holborn Viaduct (Southern Region), which is served by St. Paul's and Farringdon Underground stations.

Copies of this map are obtainable from the Publicity Officer, Griffith House, 280 Marylebone R.I., N.W.I. Size 40" x 50" cost 7/6 each, size 15" x 20", 2/- (mounted on card and varnished, 5/-). Pocket editions are free.

INDEX

44 Four pencil sketches by Beck of
the Euston and King's Cross interchanges, made after the publication
of Garbutt's version in 1964. One
of the drawings uses the latter's
device of a dot within the ring to
denote a connection with British
Rail, while the others revert to
Beck's favourite white-line
connector symbol.

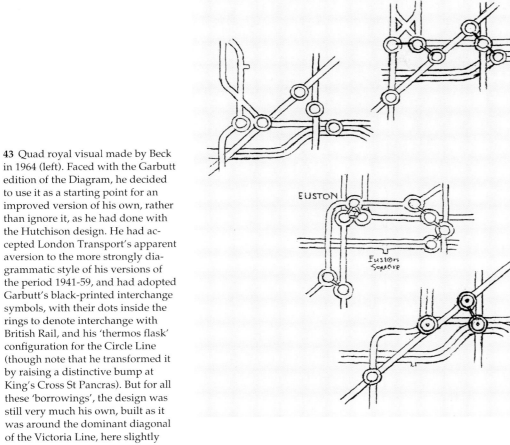

43 Quad royal visual made by Beck in 1964 (left). Faced with the Garbutt edition of the Diagram, he decided to use it as a starting point for an improved version of his own, rather than ignore it, as he had done with the Hutchison design. He had accepted London Transport's apparent aversion to the more strongly diagrammatic style of his versions of the period 1941-59, and had adopted Garbutt's black-printed interchange symbols, with their dots inside the rings to denote interchange with British Rail, and his 'thermos flask' configuration for the Circle Line (though note that he transformed it by raising a distinctive bump at King's Cross St Pancras). But for all these 'borrowings', the design was still very much his own, built as it was around the dominant diagonal of the Victoria Line, here slightly modified by a horizontal twitch between Finsbury Park and Walthamstow at its top end. True to form, Beck incorporated a final quirk that, while not in any way misleading, diverged from his usual logic: the short branch from Holborn to Aldwych ran inside the main flow of the Piccadilly Line and then across it, when it could so easily, and more appropriately, have run down outside, on the right. This caprice, however, in no way invalidates the effectiveness and clarity of Beck's last design.

only two of many possibilities he was considering on both occasions; for example, one of his 1961 sketches shows a concentric pattern for King's Cross, with the Northern Line in the centre and the Piccadilly, Metropolitan and Circle Lines around it; and similarly, he alternated between using two, three or four rings for King's Cross in his 1964 sketches.

In effect, Beck, Garbutt and, to a lesser extent, Hutchison, were having a debate with themselves and with each other about the degree to which they could simplify complexities of the sort represented by the King's Cross intersections. For Hutchison, the argument was relatively simple: could he get away with just using one symbol — in this case a square representing an interchange with a main line railway station? He tried to, but the result was an over-simplification which gave no indication of the on-the-spot intricacies of the

passageways and escalators with which the traveller is confronted at King's Cross. On the other hand, was it adequate to settle for two linked rings, as Garbutt did on his 1964 Diagram? After all, he used three rings at Paddington, at Waterloo, and even at Hammersmith where interchanges were less complex than at King's Cross. This sort of inconsistency concerned Beck greatly; he was continually putting himself in the position of the traveller — especially one who was unfamiliar with the Underground network — and trying to see the Diagram with an innocent eye. That he was able to do this after so long an association with it was a token of his understanding of the true and proper function of the information designer.

On the evidence of the full-size visual and accompanying sketches that have now come to light, the writer has no hesitation in claiming that, had he been allowed to proceed with his work on the Diagram, he would undoubtedly have provided London Transport with an unrivalled design for the incorporation of, and incidentally the promotion of, the Victoria Line. But as we have seen, there was not the remotest possibility that he would be allowed to do so.

One is forced to conclude that London Transport had become increasingly apprehensive about Beck's hold on the design and had determined to present him with a *fait accompli*. This decision was made all the easier by having the design prepared in-house by the Publicity Officer himself. Once the die was cast there was no going back; too much corporate pride was involved.

Ah, but how much one regrets the loss of the Diagram that wasn't: the Beck design that would have incorporated the Victoria Line, the only new Tube line to have happened since he first began his long Odyssey in 1931. To have been deprived of this opportunity was the saddest irony for Harry Beck.

Chapter 6

The Importance of the Diagram

Surely no-one doubts that the invention of the London Underground Diagram made an important contribution to the development of graphic design in the twentieth century. There can be few, if any, other single works in this field whose influence has been so seminal and so enduring. It has grown in status over the years, to the extent that when BBCtv mounted a series of documentaries on Design Classics in 1988, the Diagram was seen as a natural choice by the producers, and graphic designers from the Netherlands, the US and Britain were equally enthusiastic in their regard for Beck's achievement. We may be reasonably certain their high opinion is widely shared by their fellow designers.

The Diagram has been emulated often by other designers, though never, to the writer's knowledge, equalled, let alone surpassed. For its lessons have to be learned the hard way: that, to be effective, information design must start, not merely end, with its users, their needs, their perceptions. The designer's function in this field is not to supply a quick fix but to be prepared to embark on a long haul — not necessarily twenty-seven years' worth as in the case of Harry Beck but long enough to form an ongoing commitment; and that what might appear at first sight to be a brilliant, stylish piece of design in the opinion of graphic designers may fail miserably when subjected to the harsher verdict of public opinion. It is unfortunately true that stylish failure is a more common outcome of the involvement of graphic designers in public transport diagrams than is success along the lines of the Beck paradigm. Not untypical of this was the case of the New York City Transit Authority's Subway Guide of 1972. It was heralded by optimistic claims that it would provide for New York's Subway travellers of the future what the Beck Diagram had been providing for London's Underground travellers since 1933. Alas! Not so. It turned out to be confusing and cryptic, and did not survive the decade.

Yet it had been undertaken, with the very best of intentions, by a designer of the highest reputation. Its replacement was utterly undistinguished — but useful.

This, then, underlines the uniqueness of Beck's Diagram; for it achieved both visual distinction and proven usefulness in equal measure. Of course, it wasn't perfect. Inevitably, as the work of one man, it displayed some of that man's idiosyncrasies; it may, arguably, have sacrificed just too much geographical resemblance in the cause of clarity; and it has been accused, by some, of presenting an oversimplified view, not only of the network, but of London itself. But none of these criticisms can diminish its shining example nor take anything from the great personal achievement of its inventor.

Those versions of the Diagram by other hands, that have followed on Beck's last design of 1959, have benefited hugely from his original. Tim Demuth, working as a designer at London Transport restored to his versions of the Diagram much of the spirit and some of the favourite features of Beck's designs. His 'London's Railways' diagram of 1973 was an accomplished, and long overdue, fulfilment of Beck's proposal of 1938 (see Appendix L); his 'Underground Central Area' car card of 1979, its use of 'white-line connectors' at the interchange stations, recalled the work of the master at its best. The current version of the Diagram proper, developed by Demuth from the Garbutt series, demonstrates his continuing regard for the original.

The London Transport Museum gave pride of place to Beck's work in their 'Finding the Way' exhibition between December 1989 and June 1990. There is now a permanent display of transport maps at the Museum in a gallery named after him, complete with a commemorative plaque. At long last this mark of official recognition ensured that the public could be made aware of the great debt London Transport owes to the singular achievement of Henry C Beck.

45 1994 Journey Planner adapted to incorporate all known projected extensions and new lines. Beck's original concept, adapted by Garbutt and successive designers, has shown itself flexible enough to accommodate most effectively the actual and planned extensions of the last 30 years. This version has been produced for internal use. It is planned that it will form the next generation of Journey Planners, but with the inclusion only of lines that are running or being built.

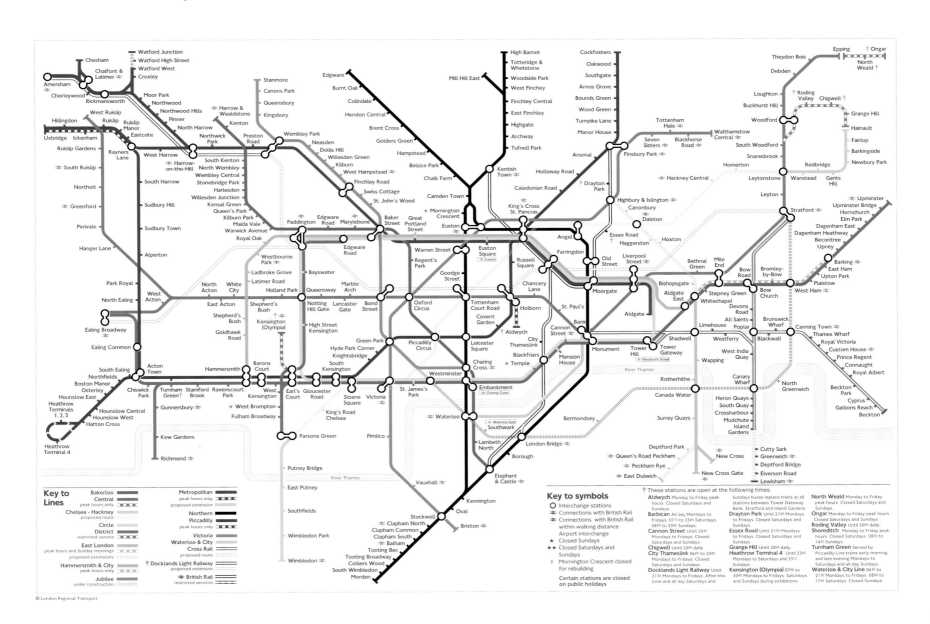

Appendices

The following items, arranged in roughly chronological order, are all intended to throw additional light, in some fashion or another, on Beck's work for the Diagram. The A L Gwynne map (Appendix A) which appeared in the same year as the Diagram itself, makes an intriguing comparison both as an image in its own right and for the explanatory text accompanying it, which supplies a rationale for its distortion that is similar to Beck's, though with very different results. Appendix B, a proposal for a diagram showing the whole of London's railway network, surface and underground, designed in 1938, provides an interesting comparison with 'London's Railways', a work on the same subject designed by another hand and published in 1973. Beck's speculative design for a Paris Metro diagram (Appendix C) demonstrates that a solution ideally suited to one context is not necessarily appropriate to another. A large number of the appendices are made up of Beck's own sketches and visuals for the Diagram, though it has to be pointed out that, of all those shown here, only one – Appendix D – refers to the design and preparation of actual published editions of the diagram; the rest are concerned with speculative work undertaken after 1959, when Beck had been supplanted as the Diagram's designer. Appendix H indicates the development of successive representations of the Underground network over the half century from 1908 to 1959, contrasted with a true-to-scale map of the area they encompassed. Finally, an affectionate memoir by a colleague and friend of Harry Beck (Appendix M) gives a valuable insight into the nature of a man whose major contribution to information design could not have been more public yet whose own life and character could not have been more modest.

Straight-line route indicators had been long established – for example, in medieval street maps – and were much in use by railway companies from the nineteenth century. This example is a route diagram of suburban trains on the Great Eastern Section of the London and North Eastern Railway. Designed by George Dow and issued in 1929, it therefore pre-dated and may have influenced the Beck Diagram.

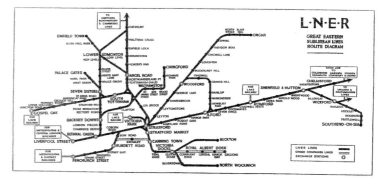

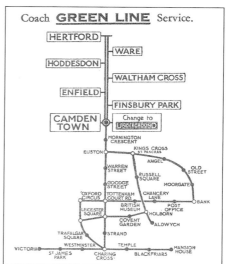

A diagrammatic map which formed part of a Green Line leaflet issued in 1930 showing connections with Underground services. Based on vertical and horizontal axes, involving a considerable amount of distortion from a strictly geographic norm, it is also an interesting precursor to the Beck Diagram, demonstrating as it does a similar desire to clarify the information about route connections by diagrammatic means.

Appendix A. A L Gwynne map of January 1933. Coinciding with Beck's Diagram, which appears to have overshadowed it completely, this design was a well-meaning but misguided attempt to relate many places of interest to the Underground network. As well as buildings of note such as Buckingham Palace, the Royal Academy and the Tower of London, it included football stadiums, cricket grounds, speedway circuits and dog racing tracks. Terminal stations of the Underground lines were denoted by a bar-and-disc symbol, interchange stations by a bar-and-ring or a bar and two linked rings, depending on whether access to the other line was by subway or by the street. The use of these devices may have spurred the London Passenger Transport Board to press later for their incorporation in the Beck Diagram. Of particular interest is the text in the key panel at the bottom right of the poster: 'This map diagram is not to scale although most stations and places are in their relative positions. Some distortion of scale has been found necessary in the interest of clarity. For instance, the scale of the central portion of the Underground system, enclosing the main interchange stations, has been opened out, while that of the surrounding districts has been compressed from north, east, south and west...'

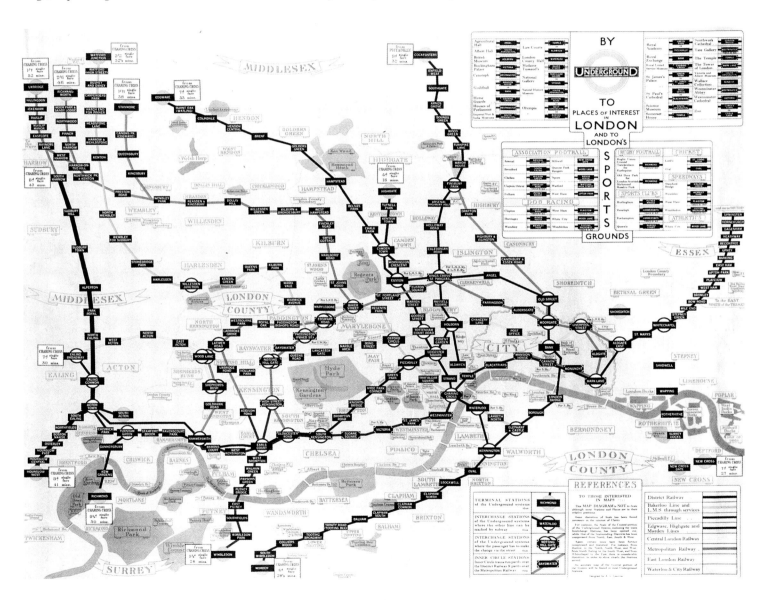

Appendix B. Whole rail system of Greater London: a proposal.
A photocopy from the original (whereabouts unknown), signed 'H.C. Beck 1938' in the bottom left-hand corner. It is clear from the key panel, bottom left, that the original was in at least six colours. Interchange stations were denoted by a diamond. This symbol was confined to those stations inside the central area and, strangely, Highgate and Willesden Junction. The former never was an interchange station in reality since the proposed Underground link across from Finsbury Park which would have justified that status was abandoned; the latter presumably received its diamond because

it was, as its name implied, also a junction of surface lines. Yet those main line termini within the central area which were not also at the junctions of two Underground lines or branches – namely Victoria, Euston and Marylebone – did not merit diamonds, so why Willesden Junction? These anomalies apart, the proposal was a most accomplished work and it is hard to understand why it was not thought worthy of reproduction. Another 35 years passed before a diagram of the whole rail system was published (see p 77).

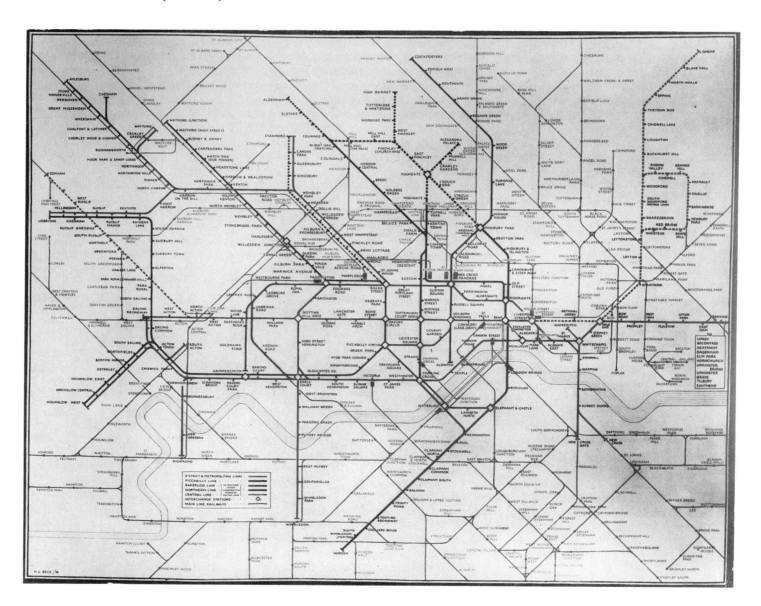

66

Appendix C. Le Metro de Paris: a proposal. Photocopy of an original (whereabouts unknown) which Beck may have been working on from before World War 2. This version must date from 1946 since it includes some station renamings not made until that year; on the other hand it shows many stations closed at the outbreak of war, lending some weight to the supposition that he began work on the design in the late 1930s. Beck told the writer that he had been invited to submit a design along the lines of his London Underground Diagram but that when he showed it to them they realised the style was inappropriate to the Metro network. Although the work was clearly undertaken very seriously and involved a vast amount of sustained effort, there does not appear to have been an official commission from the Metro authority, nor is there any remaining record of correspondence between them and Beck on the matter. Beck continued working on the design until at least 1951 but there is no evidence that he resubmitted the design.

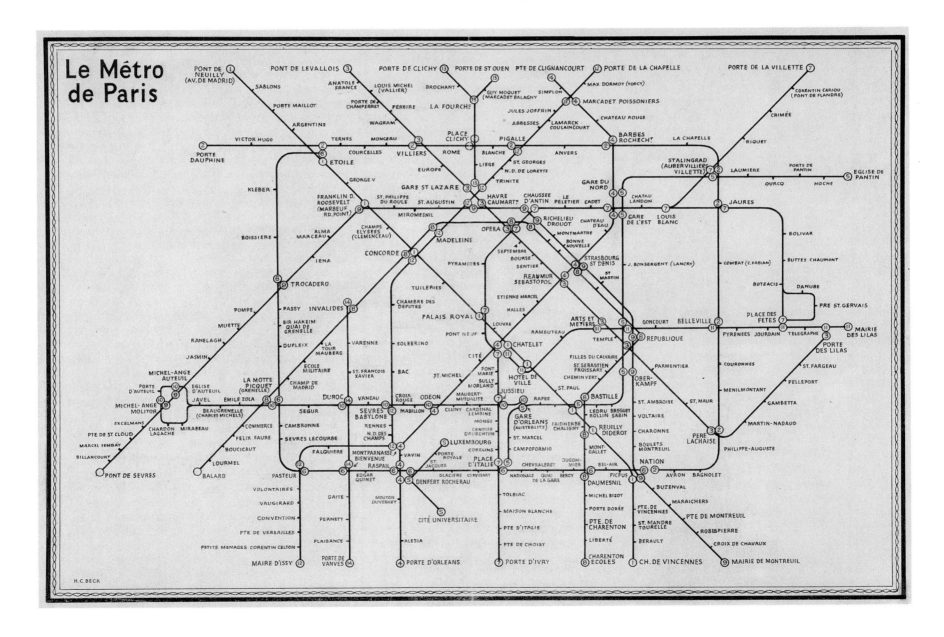

67

Appendix D. Pencil sketch by Beck of eastern end of Circle Line.
The earliest extant working drawing for a quad royal edition of the Diagram, this dates from 1949-50. With the promotion of the Inner Circle to the status of a separate line with its own colour – yellow – Beck was presented with the challenging task of inserting this extra line into the more congested parts of the Circle. This drawing shows a treatment of the most difficult section: the sharp bend at Aldgate which is also the western limb of the 'Aldgate triangle', where the eastbound District and Metropolitan Lines converge at Aldgate East.

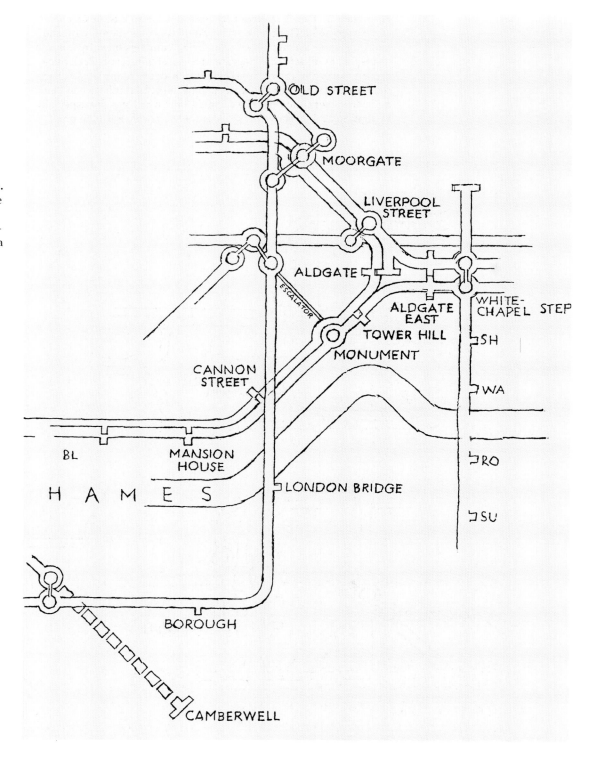

Appendix E. Pencil sketches by Beck of eastern end of Circle Line: continued. Dating from the latter half of the 1960s, when he had little expectation of ever again being commissioned by London Transport to update the Diagram, these sketches reveal Beck once more absorbed in the complexity of the Aldgate triangle with, incidentally, variations on the treatment of the escalator between Bank and Monument stations. The two left-hand drawings are especially intriguing as they show Beck's attempt to grapple with the proposed route of the Fleet Line (later renamed the Jubilee Line). It was intended that it would extend from Charing Cross via Aldwych, Ludgate Circus and Cannon Street to Fenchurch Street, thence under the river to Surrey Docks, New Cross and Lewisham. It was typical of Beck that he was eager to take on this most intractable of problems, even though the likelihood of his ever being asked to put his solution into practice was now nil. In the event, the proposal to extend the line beyond Charing Cross was shelved indefinitely.

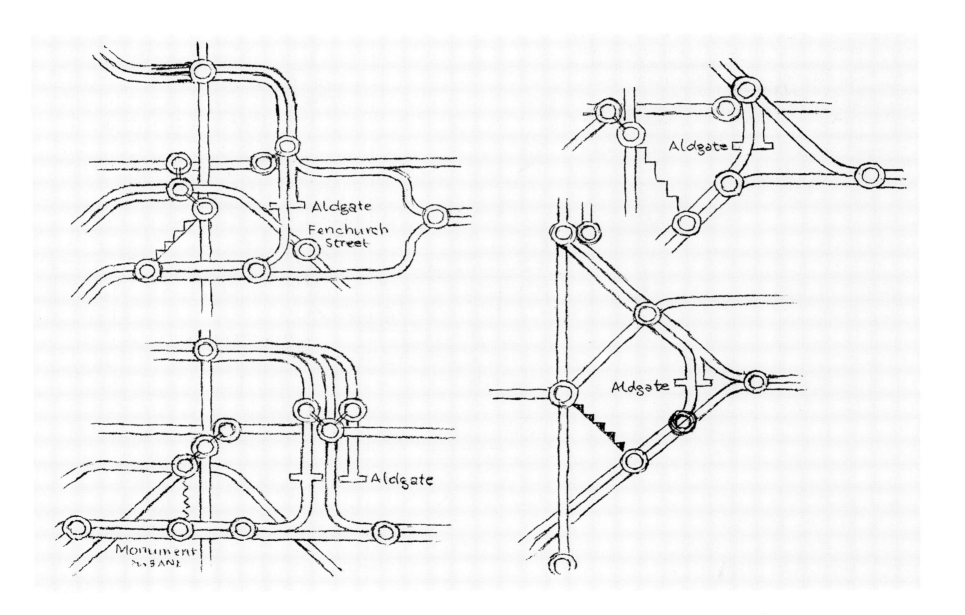

Appendix F. Fine tuning on the Northern Line. Pencil sketches by Beck of the Camden Town/Mornington Crescent/Euston complex, made in 1960 during work on the unpublished design he submitted unsuccessfully to London Transport. As can be seen from the arrangement of tunnels at this point (see below), it was virtually impossible to represent it on the Diagram in any but the most rudimentary form; but that didn't stop Beck from trying.

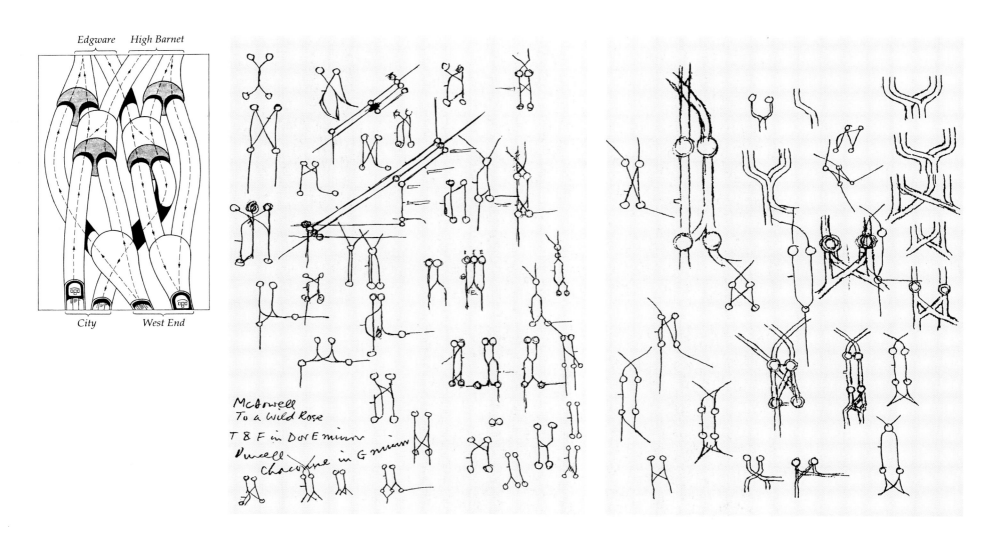

Appendix G. Pencil sketches by Beck of Euston and King's Cross interchanges. Made in 1961, after the publication of the Hutchison version of the Diagram, they all employ Beck's favourite device of 'white-line connectors' but there is one drawing (right) which includes a device he had not used hitherto: an open square at Euston and at King's Cross St Pancras to represent the connection with the main line termini. He may have been spurred to this by Hutchison's clumsy use of open squares for those stations with connections to British Rail, but of course the device was an old one, having been employed on maps of the Underground at least as long ago as 1909 (see p 13).

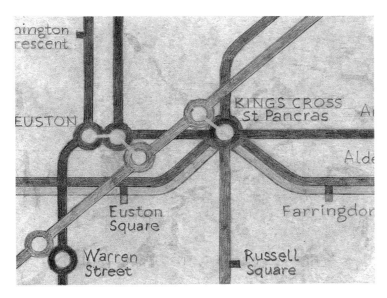

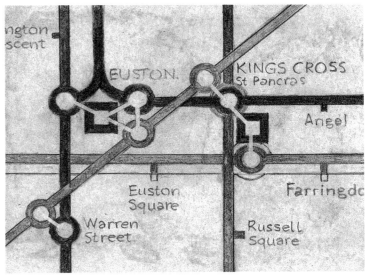

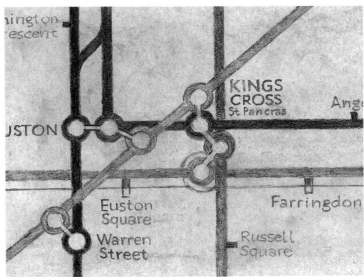

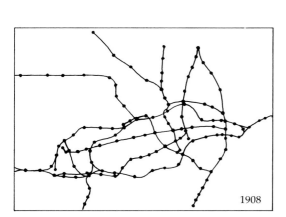

1908

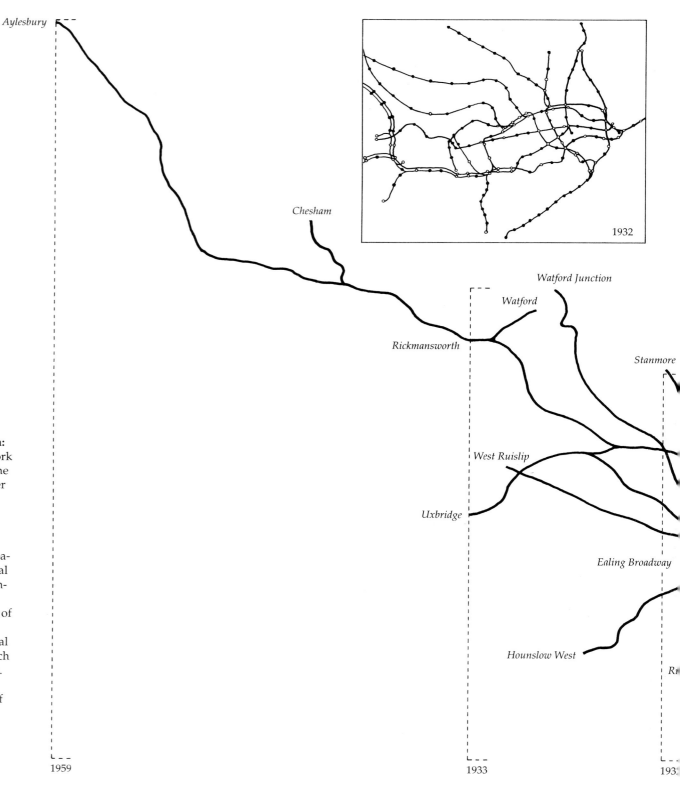

Aylesbury

Chesham

1932

Watford Junction

Watford

Rickmansworth

Stanmore

West Ruislip

Uxbridge

Ealing Broadway

Hounslow West

R

Appendix H. True scale and diagrammatic distortion: a comparison. Main drawing: the Underground network as it existed in 1959, the date of Beck's last version of the Diagram, shown in true geographical scale. The smaller sketches show the basic configurations of, from left to right: the first general map of the Underground, 1908; F H Stingemore's last map, 1932; Beck's first Diagram, 1933; and his last version, 1959. For comparison purposes, the central areas of all four are shown to a comparable scale with the main drawing, on which the vertical dashed lines indicate the ever greater total areas encompassed between 1908 and 1959. It will be seen that the linear distortion was at its most extreme on the branch of the Metropolitan Line between Rickmansworth and Aylesbury on the 1959 version, where the latter terminal is lined up on the left side of the Diagram with the much less distant terminals at Uxbridge and Hounslow West. Other noticeable departures from topographical accuracy include the separation of the southern terminals of Wimbledon on the District Line and Morden on the Northern Line, and the bending of the District Line between Mile End and Upminster.

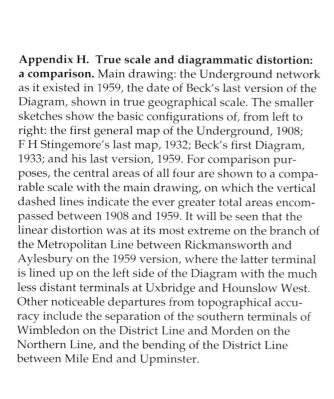

1959

1933

193

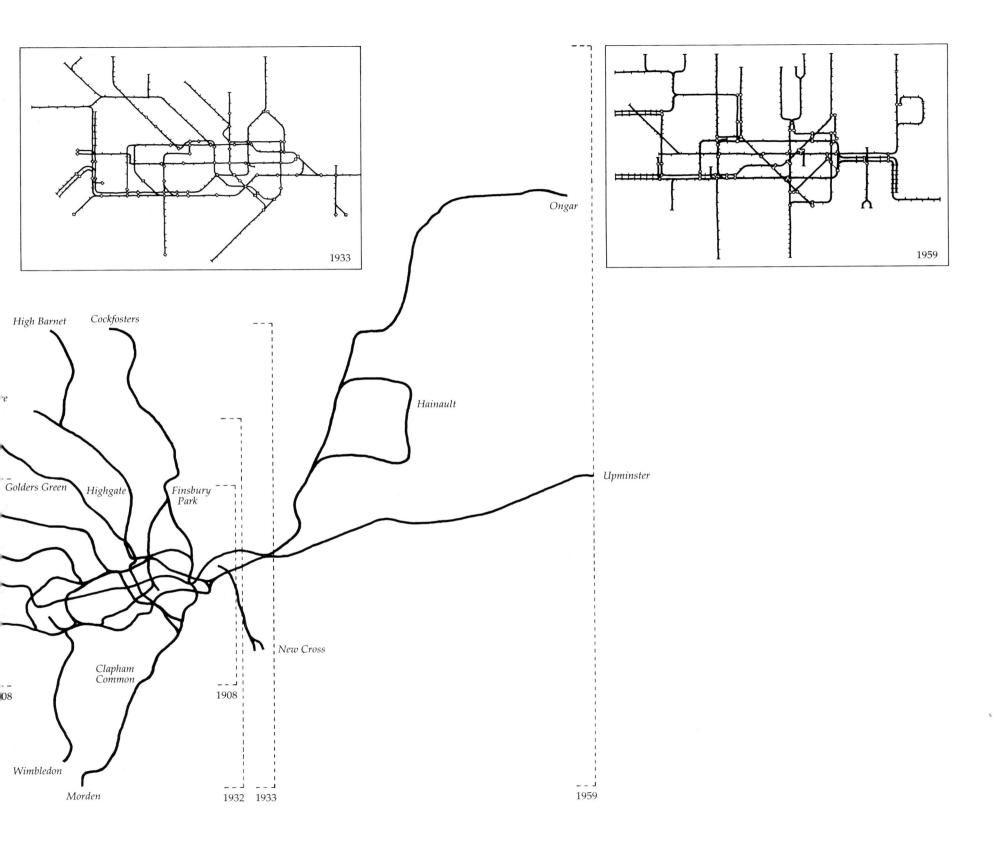

1933

1959

Ongar

Hainault

High Barnet

Cockfosters

Golders Green   Highgate   Finsbury
                                Park

Upminster

New Cross

1908

Clapham
Common

08

1932 1933

Wimbledon

Morden

1959

Appendix I. Pencil sketches by Beck of experimental treatment of the central area. In a daring exercise of uncertain date but not earlier than 1964 (because of his adoption of Garbutt's dot-in-circle device), Beck converted the Circle Line into an ellipse – as near as he could get to a circle – and produced a most intriguing alternative to his customary rectangular mode.

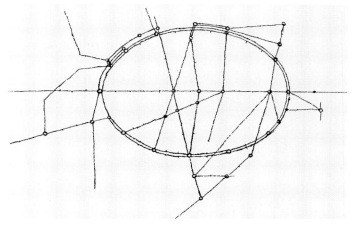

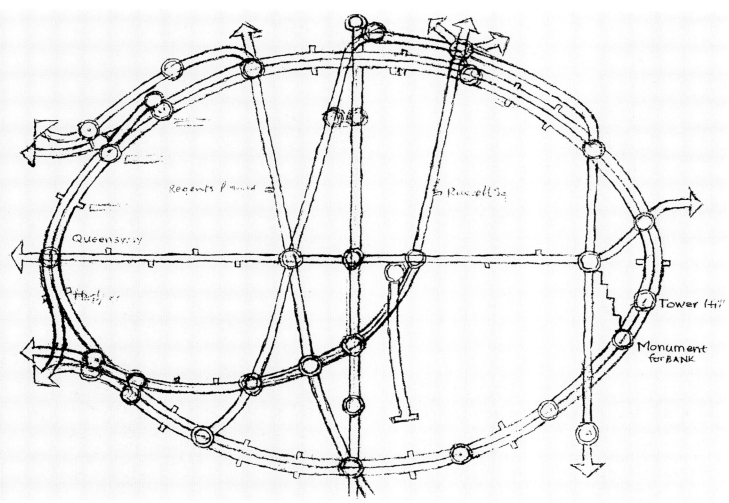

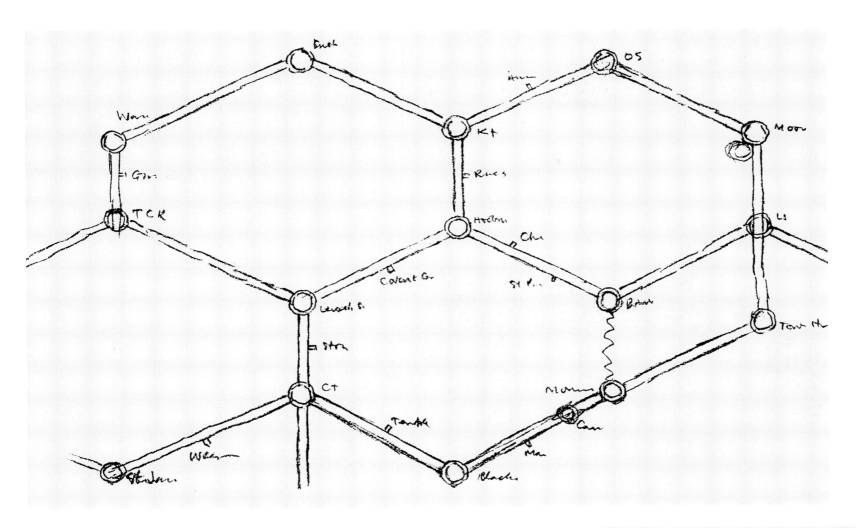

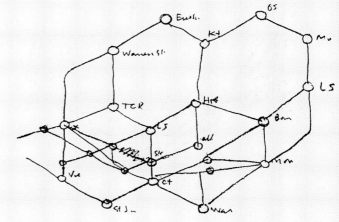

Appendix J. Pencil sketches by Beck of an experiment with hexagonal modules. Of unknown date but almost certainly at about the same time as the drawings shown in Appendix I, these presumably refer to an idea which would have encompassed the whole Diagram rather than merely the central area. This is interesting evidence of a still fertile mind; Beck appears, however to have recognised the impracticality of such an insistent device before he had got beyond the first few sketches, and took the idea no further.

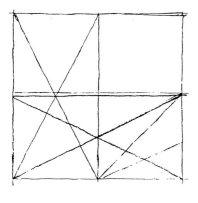

Appendix K. Pencil sketches by Beck of a multiple angle experiment. Probably of the same approximate date as the drawings in Appendix I and J, this intricate concept was, in the present writer's opinion, the most interesting of all Beck's experiments of this period. With the intention, it appears, of achieving greater subtlety and flexibility in the Diagram, he evolved two extra diagonals from double squares (see left). Depending on whether they were one above the other or one beside the other, he then had the use of the diagonals of either 27° or 63° to the horizontal. The complications of such an idea would have defeated anyone with a less ingenious mind than Beck's, but in any case he never put it to the proof.

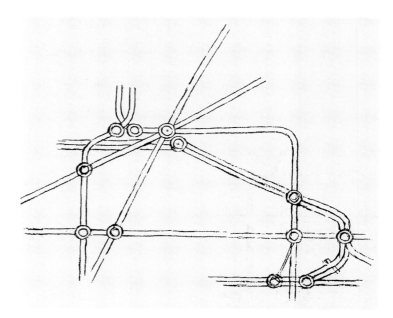

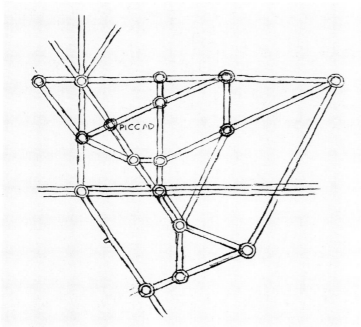

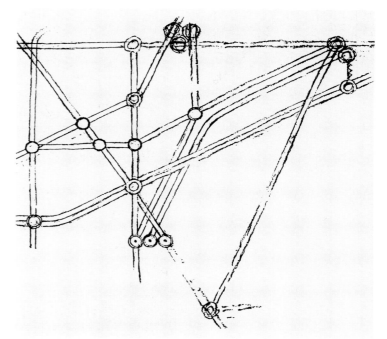

Appendix L. London's Railways: a long-delayed fulfilment.

In 1973, thirty-five years after Beck's initial proposal (see p 66), a comprehensive diagram of the surface and Underground rail networks of Greater London was designed in the Publicity Office of London Transport by Tim Demuth. Where Beck had been unable to include the whole of the Underground system – he showed the District Line only as far as Barking – Demuth showed it in its entirety; but by that time, the District Line no longer extended as far as Southend, nor the Metropolitan Line as far as Aylesbury. Demuth, whose recognition of his debt to Beck is always unstinting, says in commenting on his design, 'You will see that I lifted Beck's idea for interchange circles.' A generous attribution, but as we have already seen (p 13), that device predated Beck's own Diagram. In fact, Demuth introduced his own variation on the 'white-line connector' in his treatment of the main line terminals. This design, while purporting to represent the whole of London's railways equally, being sponsored by both London Transport and British Rail, favoured the former insofar as the surface lines were shown only in outline; these were modified to solid lines in the next edition but the emphasis remained firmly on the Underground network.

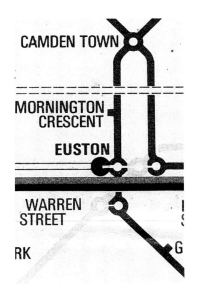

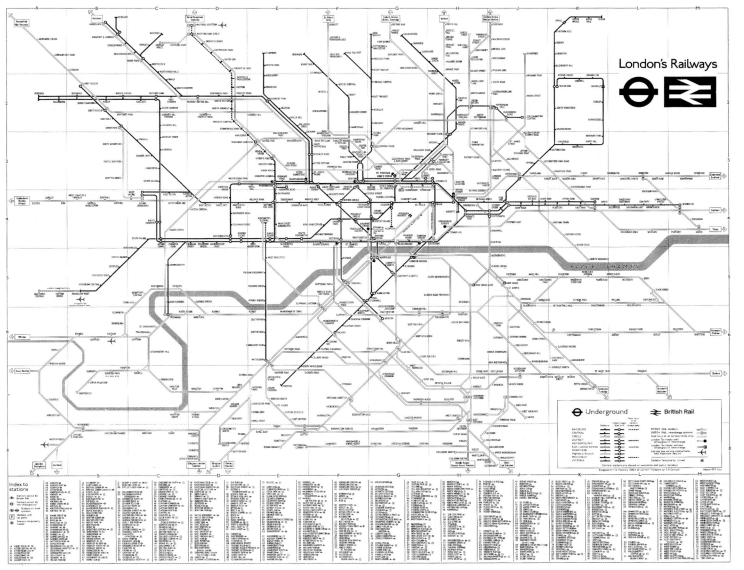

Appendix M. H C Beck: a memoir by Bryce Beaumont.

Bryce Beaumont was Harold F Hutchison's deputy as Publicity Officer for many years, becoming Publicity Officer himself on Hutchison's retirement in 1965, a post he occupied until his own retirement in December 1975.

I met H C Beck in 1936. I had joined London Transport as a copywriter following a whim of Frank Pick, who, one day, thought the organisation was a bit short of graduates. He instructed Christian Barman, then Publicity Officer, to get one for his side of the house and he, after a bit of digging in the warren of Cambridge, came back with a rabbit. I don't think Pick pursued the matter further, for I never met him and even though a few years later I was writing copy for all kinds of publications I never heard whether or not Pick was satisfied with the shy animal that Barman had produced.

On the first morning, then, I was taken to the Press Advertising Office. There were only two other members. The Chief was A C Clarke, who had been taken over with the LCC trams. He was an immensely reserved person of great but well-concealed kindness who proved almost impossible to work with. The other member was H C Beck whom I regarded with awe and wonder as the 'onlie begetter' of the Underground diagram. My awe very soon vanished in the sheer benevolence of his nature. Harry, for it is difficult to be formal in his presence, was heavily built, round-shouldered as befits a meticulous draughtsman, bland and pleasant-looking, though no-one could have called him exactly handsome. He was married but never mentioned his wife in any context. One got the impression that his was a successful if not a rapturously exciting relationship. I believe he also provided, with even less rapture, a home for his elderly father. These scant facts emerged much later, for at the start, with our chief's pen scratching away on the desk under the single window (the office was rectangular and very small), there was no opportunity for any but the briefest acknowledgement of each other's presence. Within the year we had moved to offices in the old building which gave our chief a room of his own (to our great relief) and had ourselves taken on a fourth member of staff.

Beck's job in those days was both the adaptation of Press Advertising layouts – which were done in the first place by Robert Harling – and overseeing the correspondence to newspapers and periodicals for the booking and filling of advertising space. We were our own agency and claimed the discounts then allowed to bona fide advertising agencies. Copy and layout were sent to a typesetter, who was usually also a process engraver, and when proofs had been passed, it was the typesetter who arranged for the stereo or plate to be delivered to the appropriate address. I should mention, in passing, another of Beck's accomplishments. He had a pleasant baritone voice, sang in local choirs and, indeed, at times in the office when things were going well. Perhaps, however, I remember him best for his sense of humour which exactly chimed with my own. To me he had a kind of inspired lunacy that lifted the horizons of the dullest hours. At the back of his family, he said, there was always Uncle Bulger, the inventor of the steam sundial (a device, he assured me, for taking snapshots in the dark), and many other useful domestic devices. Coming back one lunchtime from the street market in Strutton Ground he recalled the barker whose message was: 'My firm, the Imperial and Empire Trading Company of Glass Street, Manchester, don't allow me to charge for this article. All I am empowered to do is to place upon it the trifling embargo of a few copper coins'.

Arriving late one morning he apologised and said he had been attending a mass meeting of all the virgins of Highgate. 'Unfortunately', he added, 'it was pouring with rain so they had had to hold it in a telephone kiosk'. If this joke has whiskers on it then I judge them to have belonged to Harry. That this is not entirely fanciful is perhaps supported by the fact that on another occasion when a tiresome colleague was away 'queer' (this being the accepted term for 'sick' or 'ill' in those far-off days) Harry remarked: 'Dear me, I hope it's nothing trivial' – a remark that was later recorded as one of Churchill's memorable asides.

He told me, too, of an incident in the drawing office at Earl's Court, when Lord Ashfield, the Chairman, came to inspect the building and a new prototypical intercom system linking the entrance hall to the various offices. The draughtsmen had spent a long morning testing the equipment and were due for a final rehearsal when the great man arrived uncharacteristically early. He approached the microphone with the diffidence that such an unfamiliar instrument instilled in us all (telephones were different in that you could hear what you were saying and this gave some curious confidence). 'Hullo' he said with forgivable lack of enterprise. It was Harry's turn to answer yet another dry run. 'Hullo', he replied in deep sepulchral tones, 'Lord Nelson speaking, I see no ships'. Lord Ashfield, visibly shaken, continued his inspection without another word.

Before I talk of the map, the diagram that has become the evidence of a small but unquestionable genius, I must explain that I have never seriously entered nor studied the jungle of copyright laws. I have heard it said that work done in company's time becomes company's copyright, though this seems particularly unfair in that the inspiration may have come after months of thought in places far removed from the place of work. However, the question of copyright never seems to have entered into Beck's calculations. He was content with the agreement he thought he had arranged. It was Harold Hutchison, who, when he thought that Beck's diagram could be improved, remarked that while you could no doubt copyright a design you could not copyright an idea. On this basis he felt free to re-draw such parts of Beck's diagram that he thought needed amendment.

This is no place to discuss the differences between a map and a diagram. All that is needed is a reminder that the drawing of an Underground diagram is not difficult until one has both to locate and name the stations without the possibility of confusion. This invariably means the distortion of geography in the central area. The closer one leans to geography the more a stranger can be forgiven for thinking that the distance between, say, Baker Street and Edgware Road is far greater than that between Rickmansworth and Chorley Wood. Hutchison's decision to swing the Northern Line to the west in order to bring the two Wimbledon stations closer together may arguably be a service to geography but to the detriment of the design. It has sometimes even been said that the introduction of the River Thames is not entirely helpful.

What I record now is what Beck told me when he came to see me after the publication of Hutchison's new design. In 1940, he said, he went to see Christian Barman, the then Publicity Officer, to raise the question of his diagram. Barman assured him, so Harry told me, without cavil, that if ever an alteration were needed to the diagram, he, Beck, would be asked to undertake the work. This had been done when needed and the diagram had kept pace with the post-war expansion of the Underground. When Beck first saw Hutchison* to explain his position and the apparent change in policy, Hutchison, having published his new design, not unreasonably in the circumstances, said there was nothing to be done. If Beck had himself done further work on the map, that was work that had not been commissioned and he felt that London Transport was under no obligation to pay for it.

Beck, in some distress, asked me later whose side I was on, and I could only reply that there was really no question of sides. He could hardly, in all reason, expect an agreement to be honoured that was the result of a totally undocumented conversation with a third party some 15 years previously.

Beck then appealed to Christian Barman who had left London Transport very soon after the fateful conversation and was now working with British Railways. He said he was able neither to deny nor affirm Beck's account of what had been said. He simply did not remember the conversation at all. In all fairness it had happened a war away. I believe that Beck then sought advice from his lawyer from whom, no doubt, he received the same dusty answer.

From the time when Hutchison's design was published, the connection with Beck's work was severed, and all alterations were in future made by staff of London Transport.

There is one more scene to record. Several years later Beck came to see me on a largely social call. But he brought with him a bundle of alterations and amendments to his design which he had made initially to keep in step with the expanding Underground. It was not easy even to guess at what the work had been worth and it was, of course, by then absolutely useless. Beck knew this as well as anybody, but I said that if he would like to send in a bill for £40 I would personally see that it was paid. He, however, was adamant that he would accept no money and would never discuss the diagram again unless he was given a written assurance from London Transport that his account of the conversation with Barman was a true record of what had been said. I told him that this was, in all the circumstances, absolutely out of the question but here was £40 for him to have. 'No', he said, 'I will accept no money unless my word is believed. It is a matter of honour'.

We talked of other things and of the old days and the clouds began to drift away and some of his old benignity and humour came back. All his intransigence and bitterness was reserved for London Transport, and he had none for me, though I sometimes felt my minimal part in the affair had been less than noble. He spoke of his pleasure in his work at the London School of Printing where he was teaching the history of type and type faces. 'I am', he said 'writing a book on the subject'. It is to be called 'The Stress of the Baskervilles!'

He put a thick roll of diagram tracings into a corner of my office and gave me his familiar shy grin. I never saw him again.

BB 1986

* As the correspondence between Beck and Hutchison shows (see p 53ff), they never met to discuss the dispute; nor did they ever meet again.

Bibliography

Barker, T C and Robbins, Michael, *A History of London Transport* Vols 1 and 2, Allen & Unwin, London 1975-76.

Barman, Christian, 'London Transport publicity', *The Penrose Annual 42*, Lund Humphries, London 1949.

Barman, Christian, *The Man who Built London Transport: a biography of Frank Pick*, David & Charles, Newton Abbot 1979.

Burke, Michael and McLaren, Ian, 'London's transport diagrams – visual comparisons of some graphic conventions', *Information Design Journal* 2/2, Milton Keynes 1981.

Burwood, Les and Brady, Carol, *London Transport Maps: a concise catalogue* (3rd edition), Burwood and Brady, Woking 1992

Garland, Ken, 'The design of the London Underground Diagram', *The Penrose Annual* 62, Lund Humphries, London 1969.

Hall, R M S, 'LT maps: some observations', *Railway World* 28, London 1967.

Penrice, Leonard, 'The London Underground Diagram', *Graphic Lines* 1, Preston Polytechnic 1975.

Rose, Douglas, *The London Underground: a diagrammatic history* (3rd edition), Douglas Rose, London 1986.